The Mobile Life

Dedication

This book is dedicated to our parents for giving us the experiences and upbringing that made this book possible.

The Mobile Life

A new approach to moving anywhere

Diane Lemieux
Anne Parker

COLOPHON

Copyright ©2013, Diane Lemieux – Anne Parker

All rights reserved. No part of this book may be reproduced or used in any form without permission in writing of the publisher.

XPat Media
Van Boetzelaerlaan 153
2581 AR The Hague, the Netherlands
Tel. +31(0)70 306 33 10 / +31(0)10 427 10 22
E-mail info@xpat.nl
Internet www.xpat.nl
Distribution www.scriptum.nl

Cover photo http://visibleearth.nasa.gov/
Graphic design Aperta, Jan Johan ter Poorten
Final editing Deborah Valentine
Printing DZS grafik

ISBN 978 90 5594 807 9
NUR 600, 740

www.themobilelife.eu

Foreword

The modern world is relentlessly, aggressively global and many of its citizens, in response, are necessarily and increasingly mobile. I am one such citizen; in the terminology that this book presents, I have been an expat, a repat, an impat, raising "Third Culture Kids" and requiring a spouse to "trail" after my work. Moving back and forth across four continents, we've encountered challenges in many domains – cultural, climatic, logistic, culinary, financial, professional and personal. Most of those obstacles we were able to resolve over time, though not necessarily with great efficiency. For us it has been more of a "crossing the river by feeling the stones" than a systematic, preemptive approach.

Lemieux's and Parker's pragmatic book provides a handbook for the increasing numbers of people who interact with this modern, global world by embarking on a life of mobility – people like me and people like the authors. I've been an admiring observer of one of the authors for many years. I have watched her resettle, enjoy, and finally leave complicated locations and wondered how she has managed these moves with such enviable levels of positivity and efficiency. Now I know the answers.

This is a handbook that I wish I had read many years ago. Few of the readers will be preparing voyages as epic as those of the book's guiding light and hero, the renowned explorer of the Antarctic, Sir Ernest Shackleton. But the book captures for the reader some of that spirit of adventure that propelled one of the great explorers of the last century and frames the daunting prospect of international resettlement in the realm of the positive, the adventurous, the rewarding, the "can-do". *Bon Voyage* to my fellow readers.

CARRY TURK
Country Manager World Bank Rwanda

Acknowledgements

This book is a work of mutual respect, teamwork, friendship and fun. The book would not have come to life without the common vision and passion we, the authors, have for the subject matter. Through Skype, emails and telephones we were able to keep working despite the physical distance between Amsterdam and Nigeria. Bert van Essen became a part of our team. We thank him for sharing our enthusiasm and our vision, for his professionalism and his sunny disposition.

From Diane: thanks Bernard, Michele and Alex, for their eternal love and unflinching support.

From Anne: thanks to Liz and Thora for their encouragement, to Hazel and Millie for being amazing and to Ido for seeing the potential in me.

Table of contents

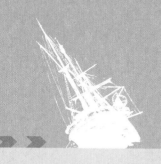

Adventure and exploration:

Sir Ernest Shackleton's 1914 Antarctic expedition

Antarctica's landscape is shaped by gales of sub-zero winds and the colossal strength of ice as it expands and contracts with the shifting of frigid ocean currents. At the turn of the 20th century, this vast, uninhabited black and white continent was the last, unexplored frontier. As Europe struggled in turmoil at the cusp of war and massive change, a handful of explorers became national heroes with their tales of adventure, ingenuity and determination in their struggle to conquer this unimaginably raw and inhospitable place. This period of exploration is known as the Heroic Age. The men who left the comforts and routines of their homes sailed to these forbidding shores not so much out of a desire to discover, as in the expeditions to Africa and Asia of the 19th century and the discovery of 'new worlds' before that: these men set out largely to test the limits of their own endurance against the sheer and unforgiving power of nature.

Sir Ernest Shackleton is recognised as one of the great explorers of this period. As a young officer in the British Empire's merchant navy he had travelled to Africa and the East. In 1901, at the age of 27, he accompanied Captain Robert Falcon Scott on his National Antarctic Expedition: in three months they covered over 1,600 miles (2600km) on skis, got to 745 miles (1200km) of the pole, and, suffering from scurvy and exhaustion, barely made it back to their ship alive.

In 1907, Shackleton led his own expedition during which he

managed to get to within 97 miles (156 km) of the South Pole.

In 1911/12, two teams again set out to conquer the South Pole: the Norwegian, Roald Amundsen, and Captain Scott. With a fundamentally better understanding of snow and ice, Amundsen beat Scott to the South Pole by one month. Scott recognised his defeat – he saw Amundsen's tracks in the snow. Worse still, he and his three companions died on their return journey, a story remembered today through the diaries kept by the men and later found and returned to the families.

Shackleton, fully aware of the challenges and risk men faced in Antarctica, had plans to regain his nation's honour. In August of 1914, he and 27 men set out from London aboard the *Endurance* with the intention of becoming the first to cross the frozen continent from one shore to the other. The herculean ambition of this goal is difficult to translate into modern terms: the terrain is, in fact, so extreme that it is only in the South Polar summer of 1957-1958 (43 years later) that a second attempt was made at this same crossing. Dr. Vivian E. Fuchs and his team laboured for nearly four strenuous and tortuous months, during which he was strongly urged to give up. He ignored the advice and did, finally, succeed.

Shackleton and his crew did not have the benefit of Fuchs' heated, tracked vehicles, radios, reconnaissance planes and trained dog teams, nor modern outdoor clothing, protective gear and supplies. This tale of unimaginable hardships and suffering, of determination and survival, is the source of Shackleton's reputation as one of the greatest leaders ever recorded.

1

The modern day explorer

Defining concepts

Today, few corners of our planet remain unexplored. And yet, the urge to discover new places, to experience the unknown and test our personal limits survives. On reality-TV, a couple roll up their sleeves to start renovating their dream home in a foreign country, or a group of young people test their survival skills deep in the Amazon jungle. In these shows, individuals test their physical or psychological limits and experience the unfamiliar in order to achieve a dream.

Packing up and moving to live in a new country is another form of exploration and in some ways similar to this televised version of adventurism. We leave the comforts and ease of our known world and head off into the great unknown. It is an exciting, adrenalin-filled journey, an opportunity to fulfil ambitions and discover places we don't know.

On the other hand, moving to live abroad is nothing like the televised version of travel. Those of us who leave in order to establish a new home in a different country do not have a crew preparing the adventure before we arrive, standing ready to whisk us out of danger when the going gets too rough. We don't have off-camera 'down time' or a safety net. Our new life is nothing like the old: at home, we occasionally drive to work and wonder how we got there because the journey is so routine that we can allow our minds to wander. Out there, in that new environment, nothing is routine;

everything – including how to get to work and where to buy a loaf of bread – is an undertaking that requires concentration. Once we arrive at our destination, only our flexibility, self-motivation and problem-solving skills will help us solve the daily challenges we face in trying to re-establish a life in a new place.

To relocate = to move from one place to another
To resettle = to re-establish a good life in a new place

The adventure of establishing a life in a new location is also nothing like being a tourist. The world's massive tourist industry allows individuals to explore any part of the planet at whatever level of comfort they may desire, from unscheduled backpacking to five-star organised trips. Such voyages have the added luxury of being finite – the tourist knows that they will soon return to the comforts of home. When you move to live in a new country, you are there long-term. Even a three-year posting is long when you live your adventure 24 hours a day, 7 days a week for weeks on end. There is no tour guide to explain local procedures, no travel agency to solve problems. Moving to live in a new country is an all-encompassing, life-altering event.

Therefore, this book begins from the premise that anyone who leaves the comfort of his or her known environment to set up a home in a new location – a resettler – is a modern day explorer. Moving to another city within the same country, or changing between urban and rural settings, or even moving out of one's parental home for the first time are all examples where an individual needs to adjust to a whole new set of circumstances. For every move between environments, an individual must manage the process of dealing with change in order to establish a new life for him- or herself. In this book, we focus on people who move to a new country because of the extreme complexity of their having to adjust to a new cultural and/or linguistic environment. However, the skills discussed here are applicable to anyone who moves from one established 'home' to another location that will become a new 'home'.

What's so hard about moving?

Some people seem to be naturals at the mobile life – they move happily from one place to another and seem well adjusted everywhere. Other people wouldn't dream of moving away from their hometown. It is worth remembering that there are hundreds of thousands of people who live in a place that is not the location of their birth or their passport nation. The fact that so many people do it, and live normal, well-adjusted lives, means that it is both possible and can be a desirable lifestyle choice.

However, moving to live abroad is not without its difficulties. We are used to thinking that the process of moving from A to B involves a series of events that are dealt with by ticking off a long list of 'things to do'. We sell or rent the house, have a goodbye party and buy plane tickets. We research housing and where to go to get the required permits; we find schools for the kids and locate the local stores.

But, to resettle is far more than *relocating* – physically moving from one place to another: it is a process in which we deal with the huge amount of change that occurs in our lives as a result of the move. Since the late 1960s, studies have linked major life events to increased stress levels that affect health or emotional well-being. Resettling is one of the most stressful 'life events' because it affects every aspect of our lives, including our social networks, our personal and professional identities, our economic circumstances and every one of our daily routines.

As we deal with the logistical challenges of relocating, we can overlook the emotional and psychological aspects involved in resettling. These include dealing with:

Labels and definitions

There are many different labels that categorise people who move across national boundaries. Traditionally, the term *expatriate* is used to indicate an individual who is transferred by his or her company, organisation or government for a short period of time. The label is often extended to the international employee's partner and children. Many subgroups have been defined: we have *classic expats* (those who are transferred by their employer), *modern expats* (those who are hired on the international labour market to work in a new, often a local, company), *impats* (from the point of view of the locals these are the foreigners who come into the country), and *re-pats* (those who return to their country of origin after a stint abroad).

The partners of international employees are sometimes called *trailing, accompanying or expatriate spouses.* The children of expatriates are known as *third culture kids (TCK's),* defined as a child who lives a significant portion of their childhood in a country other than the country of their parents' origin. A more recent term for all of the above is the *global nomad,* a term that implies frequent or recurrent moves. *International students* in higher education are often excluded from the 'expat' label though they are also generally short-term sojourners to a new country.

The other major group of international resettlers is the *immigrant* who, unlike expats, moves to a new country with the intention of staying there permanently. *Economic migrants* move in the hope of finding better conditions in the new country. *Refugees* have the added difficulty of having been forced to leave their country of origin.

The dividing line between expats and immigrants is not as clear as it may seem. Some individuals begin as expats and end up as immigrants, or vice versa. *Knowledge migrants,* (highly educated individuals who accept a job opportunity with a local company in a foreign country) for instance, may take on a short-term contract and stay on for a whole career in the same country. *Love-expats* are individuals who move to a country to join their partner in his or her country of origin. Some of these individuals may intend to stay forever; others may not.

Both expats and migrants come from every country in the world though expats are often (incorrectly) assumed to be from western industrialised countries and immigrants from developing countries. Both labels can have a negative connotation: neither the stereotyped expat nor the clichéd immigrant is thought to make any attempt to understand or adapt to the local culture or language – in reality, most do. In this book, we avoid using any of these labels and instead talk about the international resettler – the individual who moves to live in a different country. We do this because we are not talking about people's identity labels, but about the process of moving: regardless of how long they plan to move for or the reasons for their decision, anyone who moves to live in a new country will need to manage the change they face in the process of resettling abroad.

- Leaving everything that is familiar to us
- Facing the unknown
- Disrupting our social and family networks
- Losing the identity which came with these networks
- Rebuilding new social ties
- Re-establishing a new 'daily life'
- Rebuilding our identity in a new environment

In organisational theory, change management means dealing with the process of change within a work environment. It is an approach that is applied to organisations, their structure, systems and processes. In all cases, change is implemented in a controlled manner by following a pre-defined framework or model. The process encompasses all aspects of change from design to implementation and post-evaluation. Change agents are defined as people within an organisation who understand the reasoning behind a change and help realise the transformation; they communicate the excitement, possibilities and details of the change to others within the organisation. Change agents are crucial in bringing about change: they have the skills, knowledge and attitudes to lead others through change.

Instead of handling the process of moving to live abroad as a logistical puzzle, an international move is most usefully viewed as a project in managing change. There are, however, few resources that support people who move to deal with the change they face when *everything* in their lives changes. In this book we do just that – we apply the theory and techniques of change management to the process of resettling abroad.

In the field of personal development, change management is applied to individuals either to help them initiate change for themselves or to deal with changes in their personal circumstances, such as divorce or retirement. In this book we apply the ideas and theories from both the fields of organisational and personal change management to the process of relocating abroad.

Let's get started

Whether you are moving for the first time or are an experienced resettler, chances are that you have never considered the personal experience of moving in terms of it being a project that requires you to plan, manage and motivate yourself through change. Even individuals who have experienced multiple moves in the past may not be aware of the range of abilities they have developed through their experiences. Our aim in this book is to help you become effective *change agents* in order to manage the challenges of moving to live in a new country.

In the context of international relocation, a change agent is someone who is aware of and able to actively deal with the adjustment processes required to establish a home in a new environment. Change agents not only manage themselves through change but also help others, such as family members, through this process.

Throughout this book, we describe the information you need, the skills that are most useful and the mind-sets that help you actively create a good life for yourself at your new location. In this way, we aim to make you conscious of the knowledge, skills and attitudes you have developed so that you can apply them consciously to any change in your life. The 'Further Reading' section at the end of the book is a list with more information relating to the concepts discussed in these chapters.

Now that we have covered the terminology and concepts used in this book, it is time to begin your journey. In the next chapter you will think about the change that will occur in your life as a result of your move to a new location. Making a conscious choice to accept the challenge of change is the first step in experiencing a successful mobile life.

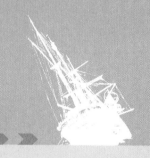

Shackleton's aspirations in Antarctica

Men wanted: For hazardous journey. Small wages, bitter cold, long months of complete darkness, constant danger, safe return doubtful. Honour and recognition in case of success.

It is rumoured that Shackleton placed this advertisement in a British newspaper to recruit his crew for the Endurance's expedition to Antarctica. Whether or not in response to this particularly advertisement, around 5,000 (!) people applied for a place on the ship. What would have attracted people to set sail on this perilous journey? None joined because they thought it would be a holiday or because they had no choice; they went to the South Pole without Gore-tex or freeze-dried food or GPS-satellite coverage because they wanted to experience the adventure of exploring Antarctica.

Each man would have had his own reasons for choosing to leave the comforts of home for the risks of this voyage, but without exception they would all have been attracted to the idea of serving under the leadership of Sir Ernest Shackleton. By 1914, when preparations for his Imperial Trans-Antarctic Expedition were underway, Shackleton was already a national hero from his two previous expeditions to the South Pole, a man recognised for his talent for leadership. He was an excellent public speaker, a key individual in defining the heroism – as impressive and glamorous as space exploration became later that century – of Antarctic exploration.

There was nothing about his upbringing that marked him as a natural explorer. Born in 1874 in Ireland, he grew up in suburban London, England. His father, a physician, provided a middle-class education – first with a governess and later in a reputable public school. But at the age of sixteen he already sought an alternative to his 'normal' everyday life: he joined the British Merchant Navy. In 1900 he met the son of the main benefactor of Scott's expedition to Antarctica and, using this connection, secured himself a place on the ship. After his return, Shackleton married the love of his life, Emily Dorman, the daughter of a wealthy lawyer. But Shackleton was not content with routines and a slow but steady career. He was drawn to adventure and travel and also needed to find a project that would provide the financial standing he needed to care for his family.

For Sir Ernest Shackleton, Antarctica was a project large and complex enough to channel his energy and desire for personal challenge. The commercialisation of the scientific findings, as well as the planned book and film that would result from the journey would provide him with financial independence; and the expedition provided an opportunity to achieve greatness:

> *After hearing of the Norwegian success [Amundsen's reaching the South Pole] I began to make preparations to start a last great journey – so that the first crossing of the last continent should be achieved by a British Expedition.*
> SHACKLETON 1998, P XI

Though he and every member of his crew were fully aware of the dangers and hardships they would face, Shackleton never doubted that he would succeed.

2. Choose to explore

Resettling abroad is a hugely ambitious project: it means leaving everything you currently know and facing the unknown; once on location you are immersed in local conditions 24 hours a day, 7 days a week without a break. It is an intense experience during which every aspect of your daily life is affected. For many, the challenge is rewarding and exciting. But for some, it can be so overwhelming that they regret their decision to move: some leave the country earlier than they had planned and others remain but are unhappy throughout their stay.

Resettling successfully does not just 'happen' – it needs to be planned for and consciously worked at to *make* happen, just like any other project. Clearly, no one consciously plans to be unhappy or unsuccessful during their expedition. But many people are not aware of how important their initial approach towards the move is in relation to the eventual experience they have at their destination. In fact, planning for success begins the very moment the possibility of a move arises: the very first step in your journey is to consciously make the decision to move.

The need to make a clear and conscious decision to move may sound obvious but is, in fact, a complex process. To begin with, when deciding to move abroad you actually need to consider two aspects of the project. The first, which we cover in this chapter, is to decide that you are ready and willing to deal with the process of change which moving entails. The second, covered in the next chapter, is to decide that you accept the challenge of creating a new life for yourself at your particular destination. To use Shackleton's experience as an illustration, he had first to decide to be the leader of an expedition: that meant leaving his young family and his life in London for the risks and hardships of the journey. Then he had to decide to lead this specific expedition to Antarctica.

❯ ❯❯ ❯❯

External change is all of the differences you experience between the environment you came from and the environment you move to.

Internal change is how you respond and adapt to the differences you experience.

To be a successful explorer means being aware of and prepared to face change during your move – both the external differences you see, hear, smell and experience as well as the internal change that occurs as you learn new ways of doing and seeing things etc. It is important to be able to identify the changes you will confront, and then to commit to dealing with them in the most positive way possible. To commit to a plan of action, however, is not an easy task. How many of us have promised ourselves to start exercising regularly but don't manage to carry it through beyond a few weeks?

The Romans of antiquity had a technique for ensuring the total commitment of their soldiers in battle. When they invaded, they would burn the boats on which they had arrived. The soldiers were left with the option to either die fighting or win the battle – retreat was not an option.

We do not suggest that you burn any boats. However, we believe that having the mindset that there is no turning back influences your ultimate success. If you begin your project to move abroad with the assumption that you *will* resettle (rather than just relocate) at your destination, you automatically begin to create a plan that reflects your commitment to resettling. You may, in the end, not be successful – there are many factors that can influence the quality of the life you create for yourself abroad (and we will discuss these in later chapters). But only by planning to resettle will you take the actions required to create the conditions to actually achieve it.

We have identified five aspects of your personal situation that affect your level of commitment to your expedition:

- 1 Your goal
- 2 Your motives
- 3 The opportunities
- 4 The challenges
- 5 Your personal approach to change

Anyone who has ever faced a project of change in their personal or professional life will most probably have gone through this list of elements, but will most likely have done so either subconsciously or as one combined process of dealing with change. In the next sections we will reflect on each element separately in order for you to analyse your commitment to and motivation for change.

Your goal

You, the modern day explorer, are considering a large expedition to move to live abroad. This is a project in which your life will change from what it currently is, to an as yet unclear future life in a new location. As we saw in the last chapter, part of the process of moving is relocation – the physical move from one place to another. If you believe your goal is to relocate, you will most probably find yourself with a job, a house and daily routines at your destination, but you may not be satisfied with your new life. In this sense, to relocate is only a project milestone: the goal of relocating doesn't take into account the entire scope, nature and purpose of the change you will experience. Your goal is not just to move to a new location, but to resettle.

To be resettled is to have a good life at your destination.

If you are going to go through the effort of uprooting your current life, you will want to be sure that you are able to create a new life which is at least as enjoyable, meaningful, satisfying, rewarding – how ever you define 'good' – as you now have. Why would you willingly experience the upheaval of change to merely 'survive' the experience or to be miserable during the expedition? To be clear, we are not talking about being successful or effective in your work – for that you will need to use a specific combination of knowledge, skills and attitudes required for your particular role and responsibilities. The goal we are discussing here is to create the environment and conditions outside your work environment that will enable you to enjoy the experience of living abroad.

We realise that we are imposing a goal on your project here. We do this because we are convinced that the people who relocate successfully – that is those who grow from the experience and live rich and full lives abroad – are those who, from the outset of their project, actively decide to create a good life for themselves. This end goal of your project is the only part of the resettling process that we will prescribe for you. In the next chapter you will fill in the details of what 'a good life' looks like to you personally. For the time being, having a clearly defined end goal is key to being able to commit to your expedition abroad.

Your motives

Your motives are the driving force behind your actions to achieve your goals; they affect what you focus on and give time and effort to. Your motives reflect the values that are important to you in life: they are deeply personal and most often instinctive.

You will probably have multiple motives for moving. There are two main types of motives. *Extrinsic motives* come from external factors: for example, a job offer abroad or your partner who lives in another country. *Intrinsic motives* are internal desires, aspirations or life goals: for instance, you may want to see the world or experience living in a different country. Some intrinsic motives may push you away from your current situation: for example, you may want to get out of your current job. Others may pull you towards the move: as in the case where you want to experience an adventure. Intrinsic motives can also be about personal gain, such as the potential for advancement personally or professionally: you want to learn to speak a new language or to advance your career. Or they can be altruistic in nature: you want to teach or to contribute to the

Shackleton's Motives

We can't know for sure, but given what we know of Shackleton's life, his list of motives may have looked something like this:

- I must get out of London
- I hope to become rich and famous
- I need to be challenged
- I want to explore
- I want to explore Antarctica
- I wish to be remembered for what I do

development of the country you plan to move to. Finally, intrinsic motives can be broad: you want to challenge yourself with a new experience. Or they can be specific: you want to get to know a particular culture firsthand.

Your motives to move

To identify your motives, use statements that begin with the bulleted statements below. List as many motives as you can think of, both intrinsic and extrinsic, for leaving your current situation, for moving abroad generally and for moving to your destination specifically.

- I need to...
- I want to...
- I hope to...
- I must...

These statements answer the question of what drives you, what you value and what inspires you in life. Once you have a clear picture of your range of motives, the question is, how powerful a force are they behind your decision to move to live abroad? If your motives are primarily intrinsic (they stem from you inner needs, desires and wants), you may be more inclined to taking on your adventure and committing to your goal than if your motives are primarily extrinsic (they are imposed on you by external forces). If your motives primarily pull you towards your destination, then you may be more committed to going on your expedition than if your primary motivations are to get you out of the situation that you are currently in.

Reviewing your motives is an important step in your decision to move: if you realise that your motives are weak, you may want to consider the option of deciding not to move at all. Once you are at your destination, your motives will also affect your ability and determination over time to create an enjoyable and rewarding life for yourself. For example, you may come to realise that your primary motive is to pursue your career. If you base your decision to move primarily on this motive, you may focus much of your time and effort preparing for and planning on succeeding in your job – you could overlook plans or actions that lead you to developing that 'good' life for yourself, one that you thoroughly enjoy outside of work as well. Consider, however, that if you are unhappy or unsettled in your personal life at your destination, it may ultimately affect your ability to be successful at your job.

Another example is if you are following a partner who has a job offer overseas. If your primary motive for moving is to support your partner in his or her career, will this motive alone be enough to sustain you personally through the upheaval of living in a new country? If not, the next section will help you look at the opportunities your destination can provide *you* personally, opportunities that will increase your motivation to achieve your goal of resettling successfully.

The opportunities

Opportunities are stepping-stones to achieving your longer-term life goals: the opportunity to advance your career in a new job or a study programme; to gain new skills; to learn another language; to put your children in a better school; to improve your financial situation; to experience doing business in another culture; or perhaps you, like Shackleton, see the move as an ideal opportunity to experience adventure. In other words, your destination offers you opportunities to achieve one or more of your motives that you listed for wanting to move. At this point in your decision-making process you may not have many details about the specific opportunities your destination can provide (these we will discuss in the next chapter). What we are looking for are the general ways you predict your life will change positively as a result of the move.

Shackleton's Opportunities

Shackleton may have thought: going on this expedition to Antarctica offers me the opportunity to:

» Contribute to the scientific knowledge of the Antarctic
» Uphold British national honour for posterity
» Explore
» Be in the Antarctic
» Get out of London
» Do something that will be remembered
» Make money
» Lead an expedition

Your opportunities

List as many opportunities as possible that you predict will be available to you at your destination. Start your list with: 'Moving to X country provides me with the opportunity to...' The items on your list can be general things like the opportunity to widen your horizons, broaden your experience of the world, to learn what you are capable of achieving in new situations and to develop crucial skills in managing change. They can also be very specific to your situation like a job opportunity etc.

In some cases, opportunities may not be immediately obvious to you. You may need to do some lateral thinking or investigating to discover what your destination can offer you. You can, for instance, realise that this adventure is an opportunity to test your character in dealing with difficult situations. It may also be the possibility to start something new, something you may never have considered before. The more appealing the opportunities to fulfil your motives and contribute to achieving your life goals, the more committed you will be to resettling successfully.

The challenges

Resettling will present challenges that you will have to deal with in order to build a good life in a new location. These challenges are the difficulties you may encounter – the ways in which your life will change that will require determination on your part to overcome or manage. Dealing with these challenges will test your abilities and personal resourcefulness. For instance, initially you will have to operate outside your comfort zone and deal with the unknown every day. You will need to find your way around a new environment either on unfamiliar public transport or by car using different rules of the road. Living away from family and friends is also a challenge, as is every step of the process of establishing your new social life.

Shackleton's Challenges

The challenges Shackleton may have predicted he would face include:

- To deal with unexpected, unplanned problems, crises and obstacles
- To cross an unexplored continent in extreme weather conditions
- To lead a crew of men through the journey
- To survive in the harsh Antarctic environment
- To live without my wife and family
- To do without the comforts of home
- To be responsible for the life of every crew member

Your challenges

What challenges do you think you will face in moving? You may not yet have a clear picture of your destination, but you probably have perceptions as to what to expect, both in moving generally and to your chosen destination specifically. Your notion of what constitutes a challenge is deeply personal – one person may be overwhelmed by the idea of having to learn a new language while someone else may find it exciting. There are no right or wrong answers. Take a moment to list the challenges you expect to face. Your list should include one bullet point that, like the first on Shackleton's list, acknowledges that you will face challenges that you cannot yet identify.

Having an overview of the challenges you will face gives you a sense of control over a foreseeable (at least as much as possible) future. You prepare yourself to deal with them as they arise, taking action during your pre-departure preparations and planning process to minimise their effect (a process we discuss in detail in Chapter 4). Looking at each challenge as a mini-mission makes the process more manageable and therefore easier to commit to. The question to answer for yourself is: are you prepared to face these challenges, learn from them and adapt to them in a way that will allow you to live happily at your destination?

Your approach to change

How you deal with the challenges of your move is largely determined by how you personally deal with change. Everyone develops, over the course of their life, an approach to dealing with change. Change is a constant; from the gradual shifts of life's natural phases, such as getting married or becoming a parent, to the large and sudden or unplanned transformations such as a death in the family. Think about moments of change in your life and how you dealt with them; a reorganisation at work, that first move away from home, a marriage or a divorce, the last time you resettled abroad.

There are three basic responses to change that are useful to be aware of when looking at your commitment to resettling abroad:

⇒ 1 The 'wait-and-see' approach: you wait for change to take effect, assess the impact and then decide how to respond to it. You may swing between feeling cautiously optimistic about change – in which case you may take careful steps to deal with it – and cynical about the need for, or end result of, change – in which case you may respond defensively.

⇒ 2 The 'resist change' approach: you see change as something that happens to you or is imposed on you. You tend to react to the effects of change rather than planning for it, which leaves you with the impression that you have little or no control over the process and feel powerless.

⇒ 3 The 'initiative-taking' approach: you respond actively to change by approaching situations of change as a series of projects that need to be analysed and solved. You look for opportunities within your new environment and feel stimulated and excited by the potential impact of change.

You may find that you consistently fall into one of the categories above. Or you may react differently to various types of change. For instance, you may be an initiative-taker when it comes to work-related change, but prefer to wait-and-see when it comes to change in your private life: you may feel powerless in the face of sudden, unplanned change and more proactive if you have a chance to anticipate change. To identify your natural approach to change – how and when you resist change – is already a step in managing yourself through personal change. People resist change in different ways: think of times when you felt angry, frustrated, confused, overwhelmed or exhausted. These may be examples of when you were out of your comfort zone and were resisting change. All of these responses are natural but let's look at how they apply to the project of resettling abroad.

The Wait and See approach

What is the problem with moving to a new destination and thinking 'I'll wait-and-see how it goes when I get there'? If you move to live in a new country and take this approach, you are effectively saying 'I will wait and see if I like it'. What is unsaid is that if you do *not* like it you may not continue with your adventure as planned. There will be aspects of your new life that you will not like, phases of dealing with change that are hard and moments where you miss the life you had. Because you were not prepared for and did not commit to working through all the challenges you would face, the difficulties you experience in one part of your life may quickly become a reason to abandon your project. Or, because you are unprepared to deal with the difficulties you experience, you have no plan of action to respond to them. This inaction may leave you feeling unhappy, out of control or unsure.

The Resist Change approach

If you feel that you have little or no choice but to move abroad, you may approach the process feeling that change is being forced upon you and that you are powerless over your situation. Once on location you may unconsciously resist the idea of resettling by not proactively adjusting and adapting to your new environment. The result can be that you attribute your level of dissatisfaction to external factors such as the conditions you find, the lack of assistance provided by your employer or the level of focus and support you get from your partner. These emotions can lead you to blame whoever you feel is responsible for the change, such as the company or your partner. You may have unconsciously given over responsibility for your happiness to external conditions.

The Initiative-Taking approach

Consciously and proactively committing to deal with change allows you to plan for, participate in, and control the resettling experience and to achieve your goal of creating a good life for yourself. We are, obviously, fans of this approach and feel that, regardless of the approach you would naturally take when faced with change, all individuals can adopt an initiative-taking approach and become proactive change managers when resettling abroad. In fact, by reading this book you are already taking steps to consciously manage the change you will experience during your move.

Commit to your project

Just like with any other project at work or at home, you will decide to take it on only if you feel you have a fighting chance of succeeding. Shackleton faced enormous challenges, but he truly believed he would succeed. At this early point in your project to live abroad, you need to decide that yes, you want to take the opportunities that resettling abroad offers you: then you need to consciously decide that yes, you are prepared to deal with the challenges of change and the difficulties of your particular destination. In other words, you need to consciously commit to undertaking your expedition to resettle at your destination.

There are no objective parameters on what level of commitment is enough. You are the only person who can decide whether you are committed enough to ensure that you will be successful in creating a good life for yourself at your destination. Your level of commitment stems from:

- Accepting the fact that your goal is to create a good life for yourself abroad;
- Being aware of the motives that underlie your decision to take on this project;

- Being conscious of the attractiveness of the opportunities this expedition offers you;
- Being prepared to deal with the challenges you will experience;
- Being aware of your personal approach to change and how it will affect your commitment to resettle.

This involves your ability to reflect on your own motives and responses to change. Being open to self-review, determined to succeed and having a proactive approach to dealing with change are key attitudes that contribute positively to your ability to commit. In the next chapter you will define what your good life will look like at your chosen destination.

Shackleton's audacious mission

..it is the last great Polar journey that can be made. It will be a greater journey than the journey to the Pole and back, and I feel it is up to the British nation to accomplish this, for we have been beaten at the conquest of the North Pole and beaten at the first conquest of the South Pole. There now remains the largest and most striking of all journeys – the crossing of the Continent.

SIR ERNEST SHACKLETON AS QUOTED IN LANSING 1999, P 11

It is clear that Shackleton chose specifically to explore Antarctica. Had he just wanted to get out of London, or had he been driven purely by the desire to explore, he could have chosen any other place on the planet – Siberia, for instance, or the Sahara desert. But he had experience of, and a deep fascination for, Antarctica.

His plan was this: Aboard the *Endurance*, he and 27 men would land in Antarctica near Vahsel Bay in the Weddell Sea. This would be the first ever attempt to use this coast as a starting point for an expedition on the continent. With five men he would cross the as-yet unexplored territory to the South Pole. The rest of the men would undertake scientific research (glaciological, meteorological, geological, biological and hydrographical) at various locations and on board. The remaining men would sail on the Aurora to the opposite shore and cross towards the Pole from that side, depositing reserves of supplies for the final leg of the return journey.

From his previous trips, Shackleton had a deep understanding of, and respect for, the unrelenting climate and desolate conditions he would encounter. However, even with all his experience and savvy, Shackleton made a mistake.

The *Endurance* was built in Norway by the famous Framnaes shipyard, specialised in building polar whaling and sealing ships. The team of builders, predicting that the *Endurance* would be the last of her type, made this ship their pet project.

Her sides were made from oak and Norwegian mountain fir, and they varied in thickness from about 18 inches (45.7cm) to more than 2.5 feet (0.76m). Outside this planking, to keep her from being chafed by the ice, there was a sheathing from stem to stern of greenheart, a wood so heavy it weighs more than solid iron and so tough that it cannot be worked with ordinary tools. Her frames were not only double-thick...but they were double in number, compared with a conventional vessel (Lancing 1999, p 19).

However, the *Endurance* was designed to sail in loose pack ice. The plan was that she would sail to Vahsel Bay where the landing party would set up their base camp – the ship and remaining men would then sail to the whaling camp on South Georgia Island ensuring they were not in Vahsel Bay when the ice froze as it did each year. She was therefore not built with rounded sides which would permit her to rise out of the pressure of solid ice – a technology which had been successfully used in Polar exploration in the past. So, despite all the preparation and research he had done, Shackleton never expected to be stuck in ice. He expected to manoeuvre through relatively loose pack ice and he planned his trip accordingly. This one strategic decision – to build her relatively square-sided – was taken early in the planning phase and entirely changed the course of Shackleton's expedition.

3 Envisage your future

The goal of your expedition to live abroad is to create a good life for yourself at your destination. What exactly that life will look like depends on what is important to you – what makes your life enjoyable, meaningful, satisfying, and/or rewarding. In this chapter we look at the conditions at your destination and how you wish to mould your ideal experience there. In the process of considering the various aspects of life at your destination, you will be defining your vision of what your life will look and feel like. Shackleton's experience shows that you will not be able to predict everything about your future, nor exactly how you will experience your adventure throughout. However, by the end of this chapter you should be able to condense your vision into a clearly articulated statement of what you intend your life to look like.

Your *vision* sums up your ideal life at your destination: it is the essence of what you want your life to be like. It is not what you think your life *will* be, but what you ideally *want* it to be.

45

Your vision is valuable because:

- It acts as a constant beacon, inspiring you to move through the process of change in order to make your vision a reality.
- It is the foundation on which you will form a strategy to achieve your goal. Your pre-departure planning, your attitude towards your project and your actions throughout the process of change will be influenced by your vision.
- It is something that other people can understand. If you are clear about the quality and style of life you intend to lead at your destination, you will be able to explain it to family, friends, colleagues, and anyone you meet. You will be able to share your enthusiasm for your journey and get others to work with you to make your vision reality.

Managing your expectations (keeping it real)

At this point, before your departure, if you have never been to your destination before, your vision of the future is a reflection of what you *expect* your life to be like. Expectations are, like art, an impression of reality and not reality itself. However, even if you have been to your destination before, your vision of what you will find may still not entirely reflect 'reality' when you arrive.

We are constantly creating expectations about the future – it is a normal response to change. Some people tend to set high expectations, preferring to create an idealistic future which is attractive and tempting. This approach makes it easier to leave your current place of residence and provides tons of motivation for moving abroad. However, you will also need to be prepared to deal with disappointment when your expectations are not met. Others prefer to keep their expectations low, either by focussing on the challenges or by trying not to imagine the future until they get to their location. This approach may permit you to remain flexible and open to all eventualities, but it does limit your ability to plan proactively for the future.

Somewhere between these two approaches is the idea of basing your vision on expectations that are as realistic as possible. The process of defining realistic expectations provides both a source of motivation for dealing with the changes you will face as well as a feeling of control over the process of change by allowing you to plan for the challenges and minimise disappointment.

Shackleton's example shows that by definition you will be faced with unexpected situations during an expedition. Shackleton had been to Antarctica before and spent 1.5 years planning the trip, and he still faced a major surprise. However, if your expectations are realistic, you will be better able to deal with the surprises you come across.

Checking your assumptions

It is surprisingly easy to form unrealistic expectations of the future. There are several reasons for this, mainly related to (often subconscious) assumptions you hold or make about your destination. Firstly, in this phase of forming your vision, you will inevitably base your expectations on the life you have now, such as your current living conditions, activity levels and state of health. It is very difficult to imagine, for instance, what it will really be like to live in Antarctic temperatures if you have never been there: even if you know it will be very, very cold, you may not be able to take into account how the cold will affect your routines, your emotions and your commitment to your adventure. You may, for example, expect to be able to accomplish more than is realistic, particularly during the early period after your arrival (before you fully adjust to the weather).

Secondly, your own attitude towards your move can colour the assumptions you make of your destination. For example, if you are very enthusiastic and eager to move, you may ignore or downplay information that is negative and therefore form an idealised vision of your destination. The opposite is also possible – you could form a particularly negative impression of the country in question, not based on the information you get, but on the information you choose to focus on.

Thirdly, you can form false impressions from stereotypes or preconceived notions of the place. These we get, for example, from media reports – stories of violence in one location in a country often give the impression that the whole country is dangerous. Another source of potentially biased information is the stories told by individuals who have been to, or are currently at, your destination. Every individual will experience living in a foreign place differently: what is an advantage for one person may be a disadvantage for another. In fact, people's 'opinions' are not relevant to you – facts are. You need to gather information that you can validate either through personal experience or by checking it via another source.

Therefore, when forming your vision of your destination, it is important to check the assumptions you make. You will need to:

- Use a wide variety of independent sources;
- Keep in mind the underlying biases of each of your sources in order to obtain a balanced view;
- Separate the facts from opinions;
- Keep in mind your own biases, focus and assumptions when finding and evaluating information.

Sources of information can include personal blogs and websites by local or foreign residents or organisations and companies active at your destination; travel guides that provide insights from the perspective of a curious tourist; and non-fiction books that are full of factual data on the history, economics, politics, and geography of the country. Beyond written materials and the Internet, the most direct way to get information about the place where you will live and work is to actually visit before you move. If possible, such a trip fills in the gaps of information that no written documents or video clips can provide. Finally, cultural training courses or country-specific information sessions are useful. These programmes are designed to introduce the host culture and prepare you for the differences you will encounter.

With the caveat of managing your expectations, it is now time to delve into how you think your future will look.

Your vision

Your vision is a set of inspiring images – detailed pictures of what your ideal life will look like. However, there are so many aspects of your life to take into account that the task of envisaging how you will live in a foreign environment can seem mind-boggling. In order to make the process more manageable, consider three aspects that make up your everyday life:

1 Your physical environment
2 Your activities, routines and pace of life, and
3 Your identity

You can think of each of these aspects by using the analogy of maps. At your current location, you have a mental map of your physical world. Without really thinking about it, you know exactly where your house lies within your neighbourhood and city. You have a clear sense of space and distance, knowledge of where shops, schools, the houses of friends are. You know how long it will take you to get to work during each season of the year. This is a map of your physical place in this world.

Similarly, you have a mental map of the activities, routines and your pace of life. You know which activities you will do on a Monday and can plan how and where you will spend Sunday. This is the map of your style of life and your work-life balance, which includes how much time you spend on, and how frequently you are involved in, various activities such as work, sports, hobbies, religious worship, socialising etc.

Finally, you also have a mental map of your social connections; you know who you are related to and how, which groups you belong to, which groups you fall outside of, as well as how all of these groups are linked. Crucially, you are aware of your status within each of these social groups. You also know how other people place you on their maps. This map defines how you identify yourself and how others identify you. It defines your place in society and allows you to move unselfconsciously and with confidence through daily life.

These maps are intertwined to make a three-dimensional landscape through which you navigate on a daily basis. When you are settled, these maps are mostly subconscious: you do not dwell on their existence. When you move to live in a new location, your current maps will cease to be useful to you: you will need to draw new maps of your life. You will be most active with remapping once you arrive at your destination. However, you will increase the likelihood of success in achieving your goal if you begin the process before your departure. Your pre-departure strategy is to draw an outline on the blank pages of each of your future maps in order to create a vision of your future life. The more you learn about your destination, the more detailed your maps become, and the clearer you will be. Once you arrive on location, you will be able to colour the maps in.

Let's look at each of these maps and how they are linked to the vision you are forming of your future life.

Your physical map

What are the conditions you expect to find at your destination? In Chapter 2 you listed the opportunities and challenges you predicted you would experience from the move. These were general notions gleaned from your initial perceptions of your destination and from the idea of moving in general. Once you begin to seriously consider your move to a specific location you will be able to sketch a far more detailed picture: the more information you obtain, the more specific you can be. The list below allows you to take account of 'what is' – the physical conditions you expect to find at your location that will frame your life experience there. Some circumstances may not be ideal. For instance, you may be in a situation where you cannot avoid long commutes to and from work. While the prospect of spending many hours in the car may be discouraging, knowing about it in advance allows you to take this factor into account in devising a realistic vision of a good life. You could prepare for the time spent in the car by stocking up on audio books, or perhaps you can contact individuals who currently face the commute to find out how they deal with the issue. Also, as you gain a more complete picture of the conditions you expect to find, you may feel that the marvellous location of your house compensates for the time spent in the car by allowing you to enjoy a home life that you look forward to. You cannot change the physical conditions at your destination; some will be advantageous to you, others will pose challenges that you will need to overcome in order to create the life you want.

Conditions at your destination
This list is a prompt to get you thinking of all the various aspects of the country you will move to in order to create a realistic physical map of your destination.

- Personal environment
  - The size, style, cost, ownership/rental of your home
  - Level of safety in the area
  - Feel of the neighbourhood
  - Appeal of the natural environment
  - Traffic density and safety
  - Distance of new home from old country, ability to visit regularly

- Amenities
  - The quality of the medical facilities
  - The quality and availability of schools
  - The quality and availability of the food
  - The quality and availability of shops and their opening hours
  - The quality and availability of public and private transport and road conditions
  - The quality and availability of services, such as telecommunications, electricity, water etc.
  - The cost of living

- Community
  - Language spoken locally
  - Local culture
  - Ease with which you will have access to the local community
  - Social life/level of activeness and openness of the foreign community
  - Weather
  - The variety and availability of sports and hobby activities, clubs, teams
  - The variety and availability of religious services
  - The variety and availability of cultural activities (museums, theatre, cinema...)
  - Travel opportunities
  - Amount of time available for leisure activities

- Professional environment
  - Status
  - Salary
  - Responsibilities
  - Support
  - Home leave

- Work hours
- Office culture
- Team size and cultural/gender/age make-up

Your activity map

Your activity map reflects the style of life that you lead: your activities, routines and pace of life provide the sense of regularity and familiarity in your day, define how busy your schedule is, and reflect the balance between your professional and private activities. Any major changes in your activity map at your new location may leave you feeling out of balance.

In order to prepare for this period of adjustment to a new activity map, look at your current activities, routines and the pace of your life, and reflect on how you want your activity map to look at your destination. What are the elements of your current map that you want to recreate in your future life? What are the circumstances at your destination that will affect your activity map? You will probably not be able to obtain all the information you need to create a detailed map before your departure. You can, however, begin to sketch the outline of your activity map.

Your activity map

- How do you spend your time now and which of these activities do you want to continue doing at your destination? What are your routines and hobbies, and how is the pace of your daily life now? How is your work-life balance? Which of these do you want to recreate in your new map?
- What are your daily habits in terms of eating, relaxing, routines, shopping patterns, travelling to work etc.; which of these do you want to recreate?
- Will you have more or less money to spend on doing things you want to do at your new location?
- Besides your work, what sorts of activities do you intend to do? Hobbies, travel, social events, discovery, study, sports…

- How easy/difficult will it be to become involved in these activities?
- Will you be able (time/money/opportunities) to have a more or less active social life than you currently have?
- What type of work-life balance would you like to have when you first arrive and then once you are settled in? What do the possibilities of achieving this look like?

Your identity map

Your identity is partly who you see yourself to be. If we use Shackleton as an example, he would have mentioned certain character traits – 'I am adventurous, an expert on Antarctica and a good leader of men'. Secondly, your identity is made up of the labels and titles that you use to define your affiliations and status in society: 'I am British and I am the expedition leader'. Finally, your identity is partly determined by how you think other people identify you. Shackleton's self-view must surely have been affected by the fact that he knew that he was recognised as a successful explorer. He could predict that during his expedition, his men would respect him as the absolute leader.

You are continually adjusting your identity throughout your life according to changes in your beliefs, your relationships, changing interests and your accomplishments, as you make new friends, change jobs, move house, grow older…. When you move to a new country, however, there is a sudden and distinctive break with those situations and people who were important to your self-concept. Some of the attributes, activities, roles and social ties that were important to your self-image will change or will no longer exist. Once you leave, pieces of the puzzle that made up your identity map will be missing.

Also, how you are identified by other people will, initially, change drastically as a result of the move. When you first arrive at your destination, very few people – if any – will know anything about you other than what they see in the context within which you meet them, how you present yourself and the labels that are attached to you. You may be the new vice-president, or 'the partner of' or 'the parent of.' You may never have thought of your nationality as being part of your identity, but suddenly the locals see you as 'the person from x country', 'the expatriate', 'the immigrant' or simply 'the foreigner'. You are the 'new person'. How you see yourself reflected in the eyes of those you meet at your destination will affect your self-image. A large discrepancy between your self-image and how you believe others see you may negatively affect your self-esteem.

Your vision of your future life, then, must take into account the fact that your identity will be affected by your move. As with your physical map, once you arrive at your new location you will need to recreate your identity map. This is an activity that we are not accustomed to doing – it takes energy, lots of energy. It is an experience that can be disconcerting during the period of time it takes you to resettle. However, the process of re-drawing an identity map also provides you with an opportunity to envisage who you want to be in your future life. You have the chance to decide how you would like to be identified by others, what groups you want to belong to, and which elements of your identity you wish to develop or strengthen in order to live a good life at your destination. Therefore, anticipating the impact that the move will have on your identity allows you to make plans to recreate as quickly as possible those areas of your identity map which are crucial to allowing you to feel recognised for who you are.

Your identity map

List as many attributes as you can that identify you and make you who you are. Start each statement with 'I am, I have, I am interested in, I have done...' and look at the following areas:

- Your roles in your professional life (boss/employee...)
- Your relationships in your personal life (parent, friend, son/daughter)
- Your achievements and qualifications
- The activities you do (a volleyball player, music fan...)
- The adjectives you would use to describe yourself (a leader, a sportsman, ambitious, determined, your nationality...)
- The adjectives that you think others would use to describe you (the manager, a great friend, funny, knowledgeable, a local...)

For each of these attributes consider how the move will affect how you identify yourself or how others will see you. In many ways your identity remains the same – you retain the same values, beliefs and personal attributes. But some things will change – the activities you do, the roles you have and the relative importance of your character traits for instance may be different. Some changes will be positive – you may be getting the job title you wanted. Some changes, however, will feel like losses: if you were working but will become a stay at home parent at your destination, for example.

Ask yourself the following questions:

- What areas of your current life define you positively and how can you recreate aspects of your self-identity at your new location?
- What types of people do you see yourself socialising with in terms of their nationality, education levels, interests, activities etc.?
- How much of your time do you see yourself spending with local people or colleagues from work, or people from your own nationality or within foreign circles?

- What status will you have within the various social groups you will be involved in? In other words, how will people perceive you, and is this the way you want to be identified?

Creating a vision of your future begins with understanding the make-up of your current maps – how your life looks now, what you like about it and what you would like to keep in the future. The next step is to look at your destination and gain a picture of how the various aspects of your life will be impacted by the conditions over there. It is therefore important that you base your vision on an accurate assessment of your destination.

Your good life

Using the analogy of maps to formulate a realistic vision of where you will live, who you will be and what you will do at your destination helps you:

- Become aware of how your current life is structured;
- Understand, as much as is now possible, how the move will affect these aspects of your life;
- Know which aspects of your current life you would like to recreate in the future;
- Have a reasonable overview of what to expect at your destination.

The essence of what your 'ideal' life will look like is your vision. You can define it clearly for yourself by completing the following sentence using one or more of the prompts below:

When I am re-settled...:
- I will feel...
- My attitude will be...
- I will be achieving...
- I will be the type of person who...

- I will be doing...
- The type of life I will be living is...
- I will be socialising with...

Having a clear vision of what you want your future to look like is a powerful motivating force in preparing for your move. It will also help you in the future when you ask yourself 'how close is the life I am currently living to the vision I created for myself before leaving? Am I on track to achieving my goal'? (discussed in Chapters 7 and 8).

Chapter 2 took you through the decision to deal with the challenge of change in general; this chapter is about making the decision to move to your destination in particular. These decision-making processes improve your ability to objectively obtain the information you need to create a vision of your future; the ability to reflect on yourself (your lifestyle and your assumptions); the ability to manage your expectations; and the ability to clearly formulate your vision. We now turn to another set of skills: your ability to lead your family – the team who will accompany you on your expedition – through this same process of committing to change and defining their vision of the future.

Shackleton selects his team

Shackleton had been on several journeys before and had been to Antarctica twice, the last time as leader of the expedition. He therefore had a solid track record in all aspects of exploration, from the logistical and organisational aspects to the emotional and psychological experience of South Polar exploration. Shackleton was known to be a focussed, organised and utterly determined man who could be trusted to use his experience and knowledge to ensure the completion of his mission: there was no doubt in anyone's mind – least of all Shackleton's – that he would succeed. More importantly, he was recognised as a leader who put the needs and safety of his men first: he defined success not just as crossing the South Pole, but to cross it AND ensure that every man returned home alive. The men who joined his mission trusted that he would take decisions in their best interest: they knew that he would make the best use of the skills and abilities of each man to get the group through their adventure.

A core group of the *Endeavour*'s 26 men had been on expeditions with Shackleton in the past. But for the men with whom he had no previous experience, Shackleton's main goal in selecting his crew was rather curious; he was looking to create a compatible group that would work well together as a team. This meant that character was as, if not more, important than skill and experience. In fact, Shackleton selected his crew based on their attitude towards the experience they were about to embark on, and their ability to function within and contribute to the group.

> *Above all else, Shackleton judged a man by the degree of optimism he projected. "Optimism," Shackleton once said, "is true moral courage." Those not blessed with this gift he regarded with transparent contempt.*
> Caroline Alexander 1998, p 56

For example, although he had practically no qualifications for the job, Leonard Hussy was signed on as meteorologist for the Endeavour's expedition. According to Hussey himself, Shackleton looked him up and down and didn't seem particularly interested in him during the interview. Hussey was under the impression that Shackleton took him on because he looked funny.

Upon getting the job, Hussey took an intensive course in meteorology. However, in his book, *South*, Shackleton mentions him most often not for his professional skills, but for the pivotal social role he played during the expedition: According to Shackleton (1998, p 238) 'Hussey, with his cheeriness and his banjo, was another vital factor in chasing away any tendency to downheartedness.'

As it turns out, optimism, the belief that they would get out alive, was critical to the men's survival.

4 Lead the way

If family members will accompany you on your move to a new country, you will need to lead them, the members of your team, through the change involved in resettling abroad. Like Shackleton, you must ensure that your crew have the *will* to move – that they are committed to dealing with the challenges of change and to creating a new life at your destination.

This project to resettle abroad is an exciting opportunity to make a whole new start, to explore possibilities, and gain experiences that are not available to your family at your current location. It is also a time of stress, uncertainty and the emotional strain of leaving everything that is familiar. How your family experiences this pre-departure phase (and subsequently their ease at resettling abroad) depends, to a significant degree, on your own attitude to the move: if you are anxious and negative, it is likely that your children will feel the same way. How your family experiences the move will be affected by your leadership skills. Unlike Shackleton, you will need to lead without the benefit of being the 'boss'. You may be 'father' or 'mother', 'main breadwinner' or 'accompanying partner', but it is likely that both adults in the family share to some degree the leadership role of bringing the team through the process of change. Where a boss can give orders, delegate and supervise, a family leader needs to lead by example and motivate: effective mobile families are those that work well as a team.

In this pre-departure phase of resettling abroad, the primary leadership goal is to gain the commitment of each family member to your project to move to live abroad. In Chapters 2 and 3 we described this process of commitment for you as an individual: we now look at how you can lead your crew through the same process.

There are four skill-sets that enable you to get 'buy-in' – commitment and enthusiasm – from your crew for your goal to resettle abroad.

- Evaluation The ability to perceive and understand the different motives, perspectives and attitudes to the move of each of your family members as well as their individual responses to change;

- Communication The ability to communicate with your team, to explain the reasons for the move and the team's common goal, to describe the process of change and to listen to their feelings, desires, hopes and fears;

- Investigation The ability to help family members formulate their vision of their future life by finding the information they need to sketch their physical, identity and activity maps at your destination;

- Motivation The ability to ensure that each family member develops their own vision of the future that inspires them and helps them commit to resettling abroad.

Evaluate your crew

Shackleton had an instinctive understanding of the character of his crew and could predict how they would behave during the voyage. For Shackleton, it was most important that his crew-members be positive individuals who would remain supportive, optimistic and constructive during the difficult moments that were bound to come.

Similarly, researchers and practitioners who deal with the globally mobile workforce today agree that certain character traits and inherent attitudes make living in a foreign country easier. For this reason, some companies evaluate their prospective staff before expatriation assignments. These tests measure certain attitudes, skills and knowledge that are considered conducive to living in a foreign environment and dealing with people of different cultures. Their goal is to test for specific traits so that companies can be reasonably sure that the individual in question will quickly adapt and become effective at work. In this sense, companies evaluate in the same way Shackleton did; they want to get a sense of how the individual will manage the personal change involved in living and working abroad.

In the same way, each of your family members will have their strengths and weaknesses in terms of their ability to deal with the change involved in moving abroad. However, while we agree that an individual's character influences the way they deal with change, the approach in this book is based on the idea that character alone does not determine an individual's ability to resettle abroad: an individual's commitment to tackling change and to establishing a new life for themselves will also determine their experience of resettling abroad. Your role as leader of the family team is therefore to support each member to commit to the project to move abroad. To do this, you need to evaluate your family members in terms of their motives to move as well as their instinctive approach to dealing with change.

Emotional Intelligence (EQ)

EQ is your level of awareness of your own feelings and those of others, your ability to regulate these feelings in yourself and others, to use emotions that are appropriate to any given situation, to motivate yourself and to build relationships. According to recent studies, your EQ is a better determinant of your potential to succeed at your life's ambitions than your IQ (Intelligence Quotient). EQ-related skills are important to your ability to resettle and to lead your family abroad. Through the experience of moving abroad you can develop your emotional intelligence, and your leadership abilities, which you can then apply to other areas of your life.

ADAPTED FROM JENSEN 2012

Their motives

Your partner may have very different motives from yours for moving. He or she may be moving because you have identified an opportunity abroad in which case their primary motive could be to accompany you to keep the family together: or you may be moving as a result of your partner's opportunity to work abroad in which case your partner may be motivated by a career opportunity. As we discussed earlier, moving because of an opportunity to live abroad may not on its own be enough of a motive to enable you to resettle successfully. Remember, motives reflect personal values and life aspirations; they complete the sentence 'I need to, or want to, or hope to, or must accomplish...' It will be important for all members of the team to have motives that entice them and are strong enough for them to want to tackle the amount of change that moving to your specific destination will entail.

Your children will probably not have the luxury of deciding whether the family unit moves or not. Depending on their age or your family circumstances, they may not even be able to choose not to move. Your children will be of various ages, at different stages in their development and varying states of awareness of the magnitude of the change that awaits them as a result of the move. Even if the possibility exists for them to stay behind (for example with relatives or in a boarding institution), they will need to adjust to a new situation. Whatever the case, their most basic motive will be to move because you do. But if your partner or children believe that their sole motive for moving is because they have to because you said so, it will be all too easy for them to say 'I'm unhappy and it's all your fault – I only moved because you made me.'

As leader of your family team, it is your role to make clear to your team members that the goal of your project is not just to relocate, but to create a good life at your destination. Each individual must choose to move because they see the possibility of a certain quality of life. What opportunities does the destination provide? How will the move fulfil a need, desire or hope for your partner and children? For children, it could be as simple as living near the sea, or going on an adventure or getting their own room. Gaining the commitment of each family member for the move will shift the responsibility for their experience from you to themselves.

In the next section we will look at how to help your crew define their vision, but first let us look further at evaluating your team members in terms of their approaches to dealing with change.

Resettle with children

TCK's are Third Culture Kids, a label that refers to children who spend a portion of their youth in a culture other than that of their home country. The label is generally given to children of 'expat' families from, for instance, the multinational companies, and diplomatic, missionary or military circles. Another term is global nomads that can be applied to children or adults. Neither label is normally used to refer to the children of families who immigrate permanently to a new cultural environment, nor to refugee children, though these groups most probably share common experiences with the temporary relocators.

In the past, much of the research on TCK's saw the experience of moving abroad as an exception to the 'normal' way children grow up. The experience tended to be treated as anomalous and therefore problematic. However, the global village is expanding, as can be seen by the growth in the number of international schools as well as the increasing internationalisation of school curricula, for example with the rapid expansion of the International Baccalaureate degree system. Exams for this system are set in Switzerland, taken around the world, and recognised in universities and colleges globally. The curriculum, tailored to creating responsible multicultural, multinational and multi-linguistic citizens, is seen as an asset on the employment market place.

There exists today an important mass of individuals who are ATCKS (adult TCKS) and the children of immigrants who have a foot in more than one culture. All of these people have experienced the highs and lows of moving abroad, (in some cases many times over) and are well-balanced adults leading normal lives – either living in one single country or continuing to move internationally. Because of this, we argue that the overwhelming body of evidence points to the fact that resettling abroad can be an enriching and strengthening experience for children. Parents who experienced resettling as children themselves and who have chosen to continue to travel transfer their wealth of experience to their children.

Their approach to change

Each family member will react differently to change. In order to get each person to commit to dealing with the change they will face as a result of the move, you will need to evaluate their instinctive approach to change. Once you understand their approach, you will be able to provide them with the support, tools or information they need in order to become enthusiastic about moving to your destination. As we saw in Chapter 2, there are three basic responses to change:

➤ The 'wait-and-see' approach
Family members who instinctively take this approach to change may appear to not respond with either much excitement or negativity to the news of relocation. They may not talk about it, making it difficult to help them create a concrete vision of their future and to gain commitment from them. Your challenge will be to find moments to talk and ways to develop their vision of the future.

➤ The 'resist change' approach
Family members who have this natural approach to change may feel that they have little or no control over the decision to move. Resistance can be expressed in many different ways, such as arguing against every benefit and opportunity, refusing to take actions to plan for the move, or complaining about the move. For these family members, the idea of moving is very emotional and often a frightening idea; they may need more support to see the benefits of the move, time to consider the change, space to express themselves and to discuss the negative aspects they see in the move without becoming isolated from the family group. They will need continual reminders of the positive steps they have taken to achieve their vision of life at the destination.

➤ The 'initiative-taking' approach
Family members with this approach will begin to look
for opportunities within their new environment and feel
stimulated and excited by the potential impact of change.
These members may need little assistance to commit to
the project though they may need assistance in keeping
their expectations realistic.

Your understanding of the motives and approaches to change of
each of your team members, enables you to gauge how committed
each individual will naturally be to the move and thereby the
quantity and quality of guidance they need from you in order to
positively commit to the move.

Communicate

Throughout the pre-departure phase, what and how you communicate with family members about the move will have an impact
on how they each react to the move. In order to get your team
members excited about this journey, they must understand the
goal of the project: to create a good life for each individual and for
the family as a whole. However, it will not be enough for you to *tell*
your family this: your family, like Shackleton's crew, will need to
be convinced of your commitment to this goal and that you have
their best interests at heart. In order to achieve this, your attitude, your words and your actions must be consistent to produce
the message 'we will make this work for everyone'. This involves
taking the time to think about the move from the perspective of
each member of the family and listening openly to their point of
view. Open communication will give everyone the opportunity
to express their concerns or fears and their hopes; it will increase
mutual empathy with each other's perspectives. Your ability to ask
open questions and to listen without judgement to their concerns
will assure each family member that, though dealing with change
may be difficult, you are committed to helping and supporting

them: your message is 'we are all in this together'. It is crucial that the sacrifices and losses that each member feels they will make as a result of moving abroad are openly acknowledged. Establishing open communication about the impact of change from the beginning will convince them that their concerns are taken seriously. Your communication skills should create a positive and supportive environment in which no one is blamed for how they feel or react to change.

Some individuals can express themselves easily on such issues, for others it is far more difficult. Children may come out with a statement at the most surprising moments. You may think they have it all worked out and suddenly they approach you with an issue you never thought of. Your consistent ability to listen constructively at the moment when *they* are ready to talk, throughout the entire project of resettling, creates a foundation of trust in the family unit. While one child may be open to discussing the future, their fears or excitement, another may want to avoid the topic all together. You can also encourage discussions between your children who may be able to help each other deal with some of the issues they may not be willing or able to discuss with you.

In all of the discussions you have with family members, it is vital that you create a realistic picture of the future: you will need to manage the expectations of each family member. By holding the lines of communication open, and listening carefully when the move is discussed, you will be able to gauge each person's assumptions about their destination. Are these assumptions based on realistic expectations and concrete knowledge? At school, children may hear fantastic stories about their destination that are based on novels, movies or pure fantasy. Giving your children access to real facts that are appropriate to their cognitive abilities is important. For example, many schools now provide future students with a 'buddy', a student of their age with whom they can communicate before their arrival. This allows them to ask questions and get to know one individual so that when they arrive on their first day, they know someone at the new school. School websites and books written for children of different ages on the destination are also useful sources of information.

To check whether you are communicating properly, ask yourself whether each member of your family (to their ability) understands the goal? Do they each have a realistic understanding of the destination on which to build their vision of the future? Ensure that you are conveying, through words, action and attitudes, the idea that together, as a team you will resettle so that everyone will enjoy life at your destination.

Investigate

As your pre-departure preparations advance, you will need to guide your crew through the process of formulating their vision of their future life. This means helping each individual draw the sketches of their future physical, identity and activity maps. Much of this is investigative work. You may have access to different sources of data than your partner; your children may want different information than what you, as parents think is important.

This is a phase in which you can involve all but the very youngest members of the family. Everyone can pitch in to look up information and help define the physical map at the destination. Where is the school; what are the neighbourhoods like; what does the country look, smell, feel and sound like? For children, their most important physical environments will be their home and their school. Many schools have websites that permit children to get a good impression of what that environment will look like. In terms of their home, even if you don't yet have a specific place to live, children can participate in deciding what to bring and what to buy for their new bedroom.

It is good to keep in mind that children will differ in the amount of information they want or need about their destination depending on their age and individual approach to dealing with the unknown. For instance, if there are security or health risks at your destination, you can tell them that no one walks in the streets at night so you will drive them to parties in the evenings rather than telling them about crime levels. The idea is to be realistic while not giving them an overly rosy picture but also not to frighten them unduly.

The identity map is crucial for each family member. We discussed specific issues regarding your partner's identity in Chapter 2. Your children will remain school children and members of your family. However, a move has major implications for their identity too. They may, for the first time, become aware that their nationality or skin colour affects how others see them. In school, they will need to find their new friends and join new clubs or sports.

Moving a child for the first time in their teenage years is arguably the most difficult of moves. At this age, young people are precisely in the process of deciding who they are: their current friendships are the basis of their identity. Losing their friends may feel like losing their soul. Teenagers, therefore, need extra support in thinking through their identity maps. It may be reassuring for them to know if there will be other new kids at their location and that these children will also have experienced an international move. If they are TCKs returning 'home', you will need to help them identify other kids who have had similar experiences of living abroad (more on this in Chapter 9). It is important to discuss with them the fact that this is an opportunity to be who they want to be: they have a clean slate on which to draw the ideal life they want within the parameters of their new environment.

You will need to look at the impact of the move on each individual's activities, routines and pace of life. Discuss each individual's current activities and routines and decide what aspects of their map each person would most want to keep in the future. What impact will the environment have on the activities children will be able to undertake? Will they have access to the clubs, sports or other activities they currently do? Some locations may increase or decrease the independent freedom of movement teenagers have. Discuss this impact and the benefits it will bring and how you plan to address the challenges. Buying the items that they will need for their new activities such as school supplies, sports equipment and clothing for new sports or hobbies will help them visualise the future in concrete terms.

Finally, it is more difficult for children to imagine their future at an unknown destination than it is for adults. Young children may not be aware of the impact the move has on their environment: their universe is their family and the changes to the physical location of that unit outside the home are less important to them. But older children will be acutely aware of what they have and see exactly what they will 'lose' as a result of the move. In order to get them to 'buy-in' to your expedition, it is important that you fill in the blanks of what your life will be like as quickly as possible. You can help them research the various opportunities provided by your destination. By helping each individual identify concrete opportunities that they can realistically expect in their life abroad, you will demonstrate your commitment to a successful move. You cannot create opportunities for others but you can help them identify opportunities for themselves and provide direction and motivation. For instance, you can explore the potential benefits offered by a new school, new sports facilities, hobbies, leisure and travel opportunities, as well as the excitement and advantages of having a new home etc.

Investigating the details of life at your destination helps make the future concrete. It will be easier for family members to commit to the project of resettling abroad if they have a clear picture of the life they will have at the destination.

Motivate

Lastly, as team leader, you will need to sharpen your motivational skills to get your family to commit fully to your adventure. During the pre-departure phase, family members will become aware of the challenges you all face, but chances are that each member of your family will identify different challenges. They may have completely different anxieties about what will be difficult to adjust to, what they will miss and what they do not look forward to dealing with. As team leader, it will be your role to use a constructive, problem-solving approach that shows that you remain open-minded and flexible about potential solutions and the points of view of other family members. Throughout your adventure together, the successful internationally mobile family has the mindset 'together, we will make this work for each of us.'

Part of your motivational strategy will be to help family members devise their individual vision – precisely how each individual imagines their good life abroad. As we saw in Chapter 3, an accurate statement of this vision acts as a constant beacon, inspiring your team to move through the process of change. Once the members of your family are able, in their own words and to their capacity, to formulate a clear desire for the future, you can help them start to form a plan to turn their vision into reality.

It may be that a child continues, despite your best motivational efforts, to resist the change and refuses to commit to the project. In previous chapters we argued that the best strategy to gain commitment to a project is to have the mindset that there is no turning back. However, it may be possible, as a motivational tool, to provide older children with an opt-out clause: if, after one year of truly making an effort to resettle, the child is still desperately unhappy, then the family agrees to re-evaluate the decision and study other options. This option may be the proof the child needs to show that you really do take their needs and desires into account in your decision-making.

Team dynamics

Resettling abroad will not only affect each individual of your team, but also the relationships within the family. Changes within families happen naturally and continuously, but a move to a new country can strain relationships and amplify communication or other difficulties within the family. Family dynamics are complex and each family has its own communication and behavioural patterns. In family therapy, families are seen as a delicately balanced system that is bound by unspoken and often subconscious agreements around the roles and responsibilities of each member. Within this system, if a working parent becomes a stay-at-home parent at the destination, the change may have an impact not only on the status and identity of the parent in question, but also on the relationships, roles and responsibilities within the group.

It is commonly assumed that an international move puts undue strain on relationships causing more frequent break-ups. However, this assumption is statistically unproven. Logically, it can be argued that national divorce rates in many western countries are far higher than the numbers of children from divorced families in international schools around the world. Like Shackleton and his crew, when they are overseas, there is no easy out, no easy access to a support network. This can stimulate people to work harder to make things work than if they were in their home environment. In the mobile life, the huge change processes couples go through do not leave much time for 'sweating the small stuff.' This fact offers couples an opportunity to review their relationship in another context, to step away from the microscope and evaluate what is important in the larger framework of their lives. If a relationship is not strong to start with, a move may be the catalyst that speeds the breakup. But for the majority of families on the international circuit, they successfully resettle and grow stronger as a unit from the experience.

Throughout this process, your attitude to the move will affect and influence the attitude of each member of your family. If you are to inspire your family, you must be willing to search for solutions to issues in order to make the experience a positive one for everyone. By leading the search for information and the process of envisioning the future, you are showing that you believe in the mission, that you will not give up, and that you are committed to making the move a success. If you are excited and positive, it is likely that your family will respond similarly: if you are apprehensive or negative, you will probably see these attitudes reflected in the attitudes of the other members of your family. Children, for instance, take cues from you on how to react to, feel towards or judge the country you will move to. Your attitude will affect how your children ultimately experience their expedition overseas – these are formative years and they deserve to be given the chance to experience the adventure in a positive and fulfilling way.

Your leadership will enable each individual member of your crew to commit to undertaking the journey. Your support strengthens the family unit so that it can deal with the challenge of change together, find solutions to challenges and help each other to achieve their individual goals. The skills that you used in this chapter – evaluation, communication, investigation and motivation – will be useful throughout your expedition. Now that you have 'buy-in' from your family, you are ready to prepare for your departure.

Shackleton's preparations amid looming war

'We had worked out details of distances, courses, stores required, and so forth. Our sledging ration [food for dogs and men], the result of experience as well as close study, was perfect.'

SIR ERNEST SHACKLETON 1998, P 2

Shackleton spent a full year planning his expedition and setting out the details in his prospectus that he used to obtain funding for his endeavour. Despite his reputation, this process was not easy and took far more time than he had anticipated. On top of the direct financing, it was custom at the time to sell advance rights to any commercial spin-offs the expedition would produce such as a book, a film and photographs, and a lecture tour. He was creative with fund-raising: he obtained grants from private individuals and the British Government as well as the Royal Geographical Society, to name a few. Public schools in England and Scotland began fund-raising projects to support the purchase of the dog-sledging teams – which gained him not only financial support but also a nation's moral and emotional support in the process. Once the bulk of his financing was in place, he went about obtaining supplies.

Even though he had been to Antarctica before, he sought professional advice to identify the resources he needed. Shackleton's plan entailed two boats, fifty-six men, 100 dogs and a battery of scientific equipment. He needed supplies to get to

Antarctica (including enough coal to steam the ship), and materials, food etc. he would need for the small party of men who would cross the continent on skis and dog sledges as well as those who remained on board doing their scientific experiments. He also had to calculate everything the men would need aboard the Aurore, the second ship whose crew would meet the expedition on the far side of the Antarctic continent.

His preparations were thorough: he purchased sledges in Norway and tested specially designed tents; he bought the latest and best technology, including Burberry coats and reindeer-hide sleeping bags, boots and mittens.

After months of planning and preparations, the *Endurance* left London on 1 August 1914, amidst growing turmoil in Europe. On 4 August in Southend, Shackleton read of the general mobilisation for what would become World War I. After meeting with the crew, he sent a telegram to the Admiralty offering the services of the ship and all her men for the war effort. At the very last moment, hours before his departure and after one and a half years of preparations, Shackleton had to consider the possibility of not even beginning his journey!

In his book *South* (1998), Shackleton says, 'We only asked that... the expedition might be considered as a single unit, so as to preserve its homogeneity.' However, their suspense was short-lived. Within an hour Winston Churchill, First Lord of the Admiralty at the time, sent a curt reply: *Proceed*.

And so, on 8 August 1914, Shackleton sailed from Plymouth to Buenos Aires for final preparations. At 10:30 on 26 October, the *Endurance* set sail for Georgia Island, the last inhabited outpost before the South Polar Region – the voyage had finally begun. In his diary, Shackleton notes with apparent relish '...now comes the actual work itself...the fight will be good.' (quoted in Lansing 1999, p 23)

5

Prepare to set sail

Now that you have consciously decided to undertake your expedition, you can begin planning your journey. The time between your decision to leave and your actual departure – whether that is a few weeks or many months – is a transition period. It is both the beginning of your adventure and the end of the current chapter in your life. This is when life as you know it begins to change: a portion of your day will be spent planning and making arrangements for your future as, simultaneously, you begin to extricate yourself from your current physical, identity and activity maps.

In this chapter we look at both aspects of your pre-departure preparations: planning for the future and closing up the past. First we look at the importance of determining which resources you will need to achieve your vision; to list the resources you have as well as the ones you still need to obtain, and make a plan for obtaining what you need. Then we discuss the development of your exit plan so that by the time you leave, everything and everyone is prepared for your departure.

Assess your resource needs

What do you need in order to achieve your goal? You will have obvious basic requirements: a home, maybe a car and a school for your children. However, in order for your expedition to be a success, you will need to evaluate your resource needs in relation to your goal: you are not moving abroad just to live in a new place but to create an enjoyable life. You, like Shackleton, need to identify the resources and support you already have that will help you resettle and what resource gaps remain that may hold you back in achieving your goal.

The resources and resource gaps that you identify provide a basis for forming an action plan for obtaining the resources you do not yet have. Like Shackleton's prospectus, this exercise will not only help you get an overview of your existing resources and requirements, it will also enable you to explain clearly to others what you need and why. This resource analysis will be useful to you both during the pre-departure phase you are now in as well as during the early period at your destination as you settle-in to your new environment.

Identify your needs

Because of the complexity of an international move, it is most useful to divide your resource planning into three phases. Firstly, there are the resources you need to actually move from one location to another. For example, during the transfer you will need logistical resources, information and financing to transfer your belongings.

The next stage is the early period after your arrival. You must take into account the fact that during this stage you may not have all of your personal belongings with you, you may be in temporary accommodation for a while, the local food you will eat may not be what you are used to etc. You will need to consider which physical resources you will need to ease this transition phase, such as household items and the children's favourite toys. Also consider the assistance you will require from colleagues, acquaintances and local officials for example. Who can you already mobilise to help you in your initial period at your destination? Time (to get settled, to house hunt) is also a resource you may want to secure.

Finally, review the resources you will need to accomplish your longer-term goal to have an enjoyable and rewarding life. What are the resources you must bring with you or need to obtain in order to create the life you defined for yourself in your vision? For example, if you are accompanying your partner who has a job overseas and you intend to work, do you need a work permit? How do you go about obtaining one? How difficult is it and whose help do you need? In other words, you will need to undertake a systematic review of what you need, what you have and what you have yet to obtain to enable you to eventually be able to enjoy the ideal life you defined for yourself in your vision.

For each of the three stages of your journey – pre-departure, arrival and longer-term – think of the resources you currently have and those you still need to obtain that can help you reach your goal. Your list should include:

- Financial resources
    - Income (current and future, yours and your partner's...)
    - The relocation package provided by your employer – allowances for transfer, furniture removals, temporary housing etc.
    - Other financial resources

- Support and knowledge networks
    - Your employer or university relocation/HR departments
    - Your manager and colleagues (old and new)
    - School / university councillors
    - Social groups and activities
    - Your partner, family and friends
    - Social and professional networks

➤ Physical resources
  ➤ Your belongings
  ➤ Elements of the local environment at your destination, such as access to sporting facilities

Identify the resources you don't yet have
Now, using the same list above, look at the resources you do not have that may hinder you from eventually experiencing the life you aim to create. Resources include information (such as a pre-departure visit to your destination to fact find), skills (such as learning the language, taking a culture course, or studying a new subject) and physical or financial requirements (such as financing or specialised equipment for a new sport). Time is also a resource: time to settle in, time to return home for a special event, time for leisure activities.

One resource you should take into account is country, cultural or orientation training opportunities for you and your family. Research shows that only a percentage of employees and their partners who are offered such training by their employer on a voluntary basis take up the opportunity. One reason for the lack of interest is that training which is offered during the pre-departure period does not seem relevant – people are busy planning and preparing logistically for the move and finding the time for such a training is difficult to do. Once they arrive at their destination, many employees feel that their first hand experiences are more valuable than a formal course. Not all courses are equal, but we feel that a well-designed training programme is a valuable resource.

When you first arrive at your destination, will you need assistance in meeting certain people who can show you around or introduce you to a particular network such as a religious or cultural group? Would you benefit from a cultural introduction to the country or an orientation session in the city where you will live? Will there be a long wait before your belongings arrive and if so, what do you need to make your house feel like home? Will you be able to bring all your belongings with you; do you have the freight allowance you need to make this possible? Are you aware of any special products that are not available on location that you could bring with you to make your daily life feel more 'normal'?

Take time to think about this list of resources in terms of your team members. Does your partner have a clear list of requirements? If you have children, you will need to help them think through the list of things they need in order to have that happy life at their destination. Children may want to take something with them that is unusable – ice-skates to a tropical country for instance. If at all possible, let them bring what they want: the skates may not be a useful resource but they may be an invaluable reminder of home and of a past (and perhaps future) identity.

Obtain what you need

How do you plan to obtain the resources you do not have?

Consider the following questions:

➤ Who is in a position to help you get the resources you need? For instance, can you or your partner's HR department finance a pre-departure visit, a cultural introduction or an orientation programme? Is there someone who has the knowledge or experience to provide you with information or assistance?

➤ What actions can you take to get these resources? For example, do you need to pay for extra freight allowance yourself in order to ensure that you have what you need? Do you need to negotiate with someone to obtain resources?

For some readers, a key contact will be a person in authority such as your employer, the human resources personnel or a student counsellor. For those who are moving in order to join a partner, your negotiation process may primarily be with your partner. You will need to be clear with him or her about what you need and come up with ways of obtaining those resources you do not have. Approaching someone to request resources may seem unreasonable or feel like a weakness on your behalf. However, this resource analysis you have created is a clear statement that represents an objective review of your move as a project and which can form the basis for any discussions and negotiations you have. Your goal, which is clearly stated at the top of the 'prospectus' of your expedition – *to have a good life at your destination –*, makes clear business sense. If you are travelling with your family, you are negotiating on behalf of the needs of your whole family. There are financial implications to you and your team members being happy: if you are properly resettled at your destination you will be better able to achieve the work, study or role you are to play there. If your family is well re-settled, you will not have to worry about their well-being. Your 'prospectus', therefore, enables you to have a meaningful discussion with your employer / education advisor / resource provider based on tangible project-based 'resource needs'.

During these discussions keep in mind the fact that:

- The person you are speaking to may never have resettled abroad. They may therefore not understand the emotional and psychological process involved;
- Local managers at your destination may not be aware of the issues an incoming person faces in moving and adjusting to their country;
- No one will be aware of your personal vision, or specific situation, that creates your own resource gaps and requirements.

It is up to you to explain what your requirements are in order to achieve your goal. If you have the resources you need, you will be more effective in your work or study and be able to adjust to your new life more quickly. This is a discussion you can have now, before your departure, as well as later, once you've been on location for a while and have had time to assess your needs in the face of reality.

Ensure a healthy goodbye

So far in this book we have been looking to the future, preparing mentally for life at your destination. However, this period of transition is also the time to create a healthy ending to your current life. One of the challenges you will face during this pre-departure period is to find a balance between on the one hand the excitement and stress of preparing for your future, and on the other hand, dealing with the realities of your current life and the emotional demands of leaving the people, places and activities you knew so well. This process is a delicate balancing act. If you start to pack too early, you may limit your ability to lead a normal life; if you are solely focussed on the future, current friends and family may feel abandoned before you physically depart. But leaving your preparations to the last minute may not give you enough time to plan adequately for your future life.

Though this period of transition is hectic and stressful, you need to consciously take time to emotionally close this phase in your life in order to be able to fully invest in making the new place 'home'. We are not talking about severing the ties to your current life, but about making a clean slate so that all your affairs, including your social and emotional ties, are in order. Technically, when you return, you should be able to re-build the maps of your current life.

In his book, *Transitions* (1991), William Bridges defines three phases involved in bringing your current life to a close:

- Dismantling
  (ending your physical and logistical ties)

- Disengaging
  (saying goodbye emotionally)

- Dis-identifying
  (accepting that you no longer have a future here)

Dismantling
Dismantling your current life is what most pre-departure 'to do' lists are about. To dismantle your current life is to focus on the multitude of logistical aspects of relocating. As Shackleton's example shows, there is a lot of planning to be done. You need to prepare to leave your physical home and social networks, end contracts, memberships and services, and manage finances. Appendix 1 is a useful checklist to get you started in this process. Though it may seem unending, dismantling your current situation is a step-by-step process with a clear target – your departure date.

Disengaging
Disengaging is the process of managing emotional ties and saying goodbye to everyone who populates your social map. This process

isn't about wiping your social map clean – it's about turning your map into an island and creating clear bridges to your future life. Precisely what steps you take to disengage is personal; what is important is that you consciously manage this process for three reasons.

Firstly, it allows you to actively close up your social networks, gives you a sense of completion, and gives you room to begin again with a new network. Ceremonies and rituals are important as a way of marking changes in our lives. Hosting an event to celebrate the beginning of your adventure and underline the end of your current relationships, as you know them, is a very good way to mark this change.

Secondly, this is the time when you can establish communication links with people you want to stay in touch with and manage the expectations of family and friends who will not be travelling with you. You can, for instance, discuss how you will communicate and how often you will see each other.

Thirdly, saying goodbye enables the people who will be staying behind to deal with the empty space that your departure will create. Your ability to listen to, acknowledge and deal with the concerns and emotions of family and friends is vital for both them and you in this process of disengagement.

Dis-identifying

The last aspect of creating closure is *dis-identification*. As you wind down your participation in your social networks, you may find yourself focusing more on the future in your new location and less on the news and events in your current one. Many of the ties that make up your identity begin to change as you step out of roles and responsibilities you previously had. This can be painful when you become aware of people making plans for events to which you are not invited because you will no longer be around.

The process of dis-identification happens over a longer period of time and may be complete only after you have lived in your new location for some time. Perhaps you will notice it when you return to what used to be your home for a holiday – you may catch yourself using the word 'home' in reference to your new location or see old activities and networks with a detached, uninvolved eye. The extent to which you will be able to fully engage in your adventure will certainly be affected by how effectively you dismantle, disengage and dis-identify with your current life.

Facilitate your family's preparations for their departure

Your partner will need to prepare for his or her own departure. If they are not reading this book, you may want to discuss the process with them and ensure that they are aware of and actively engaged in the process. Some of the activities and discussions you will do together for mutual friends or joint activities. However, because the pre-departure period is busy and stressful, it is easy to overlook the fact that children need to be guided through the process of dismantling, disengaging and dis-identifying with their environment as well. Giving children a say in their preparations for leaving is an important way in which you give them some control over the transition process.

Dismantling

Even young children can be asked their opinion about what they want to take along, either in a shipment or in a suitcase, even if you know that they won't be able to use that item in the next location. Engage children in the discussion about the clubs and organisations they will stop attending. Some subscriptions to magazines, for instance, can be continued if it is possible to send them on to your destination. You could also give your children the chance to personally tell teachers and classmates that they are leaving, with you present as support.

Disengaging

Involve the children in the process of saying goodbye to their friends and family members. You can help them send out change of address cards and gather address information of their friends. Help them set up a means of communication with friends (set up an email or Skype account for example). You can involve them in the process of organising a going away celebration.

Not all children may want to do this, but if they do, mark every 'last time', for instance 'the last time we go to the park', so that children can say goodbye to places and routines in their lives and be conscious of endings. For those children who take a 'wait and see' approach, being aware of endings will help them focus more on the future. Discuss with them how supportive or understanding people in their environment are (or are not). How do their friends feel about their moving away? Are they angry, uninterested or shocked? What can you do to make the environment positive if it isn't already? You or your children can provide a presentation on their destination so that they can share with friends and classmates what they know about their future 'home'. Talk about opportunities like a return visit, keeping in touch or possible holidays together.

Dis-identifying

As the time to leave draws near, children will notice that they are no longer a part of the future activities of their classmates and friends: plans for next week or next year will not include them. Talking with children about what can be a painful process will help them understand it. How they feel is as normal as it is unpleasant. Here you can play an important role in helping them begin to identify with the new place: they will still be a student in a classroom and that class will have other plans that they will be a part of; they will make friends with whom they will do other activities.

And now for the great leap

In the first part of this chapter you undertook a 'needs assessment' listing your resources and resource gaps, and you created a 'prospectus' of your expedition that articulates a clear vision and plan of how to obtain the resources you need for a successful journey. You also devised a plan for negotiating and obtaining 'buy-in' from others to ensure their support for your efforts. An assertive and determined attitude to your project will be most helpful in achieving your goal.

In the second section of this chapter, we took you through the process of emotionally, psychologically and logistically disengaging from your current life, as well as leading your family members through this process. This requires self-knowledge, empathy with others, communication skills, as well the ability to manage your time in order to balance the demands of your current and future networks.

In the pre-departure phase of resettling you can experience both excitement for the future and sadness for what is ending. As with many of life's major events, there is a familiar emotional pattern that most people go through. The phase of forming your vision for the future is often experienced as a positive, exciting time. As the moment of departure approaches, particularly in the period of saying goodbye to friends and family and moving out of one's home, doubt about the decision can begin to surface. Often individuals notice the small things that they will miss – even the things they usually dislike. It can create a wave of nostalgia. It is as if your life is placed under a microscope and details become magnified and take on an unnaturally large importance. The last days before departure are often chaotic, and the very last day can feel surreal. However, the day will come when you take your suitcases, board that 'ship', and leave home. The decision has been taken, everything has been taken care of and you can now 'relax' and look towards the future.

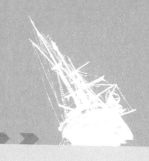

Shackleton faces unusual Antarctic conditions

On 5 December 1914, the *Endurance* sailed from South Georgia Island, the crew's last link with civilisation. For the next four weeks the ship dodged icebergs, smashed through young ice three feet thick (one meter), glanced off solid shoals of older ice, and hurtled down narrow leads between icebergs that quickly opened and closed in a jigsaw puzzle of ice that stretched as far as the eye could see.

> *Steering in these conditions required muscle as well as nerve...I had been prepared for evil conditions in the Weddell Sea, but had hoped that in December and January, at any rate, the pack would be loose, even if no open water was to be found. What we were actually encountering was fairly dense pack of a very obstinate character.*
> Shackleton 1998, p 10

On 19 January 1915, within view of land, a long and unusually violent storm froze the ice around the ship into a solid pack, something Shackleton had not expected so early in the season. In the days that followed, the weather improved and Shackleton and his men used all their ingenuity, steam power and human strength to wriggle the ship out of the ice pack and into patches of open water. Eventually, however, there was no more water to be seen, in any direction. They found themselves frozen, drifting fortuitously though painstakingly slowly, in their intended direction. On 22 February they reached a point 16 nautical miles off the shore – a one-day sail under normal conditions to their landing destination. But then the strong ocean currents swirled in their natural pattern along the shore and the *Endurance* started moving north again within the ice pack.

At this point, Sir Ernest Shackleton would have realised that he would not even begin his journey across Antarctica. He must have been enormously disappointed. On 24 February he assembled his men. In their journals, several members describe the way he addressed them with the momentous news that their transcontinental expedition was over. He showed no outward sign of disappointment or anger. He explained their predicament, told them of the various possibilities the future might hold, and then got down to organising their lives for the coming months. His diary shows his understated, rational state of mind:

> *My chief anxiety is the drift. Where will the vagrant winds and currents carry the ship during the long winter months that are ahead of us? We will go west, no doubt, but how far? And will it be possible to break out of the pack early in the spring and reach Vahsel Bay or some other suitable landing-place? These are momentous questions for us.*
> SHACKLETON 1998, P 36

Shackleton knew of the dangers of the long, desolately dark months of the Antarctic winter: boredom and tedium led to irritations and depression. To guard against this, he set up a strict routine. There were hours dedicated to ship maintenance and work, to dog care and to personal exercise and leisure. Their most important task was to collect a large supply of meat for men and dogs, and blubber for fuel, so hunting parties were organised.

For eight months they lived on board. Shackleton divided dogs and men into six teams, which inevitably led to races and team rivalries that focussed minds and energy for several hours each day. In the evenings there were sing-alongs, board games and storytelling sessions. The sun gradually disappeared and was not seen again for four long months.

6 New territory

Here you are, feet firmly planted on the shores of your new home. You are now fully immersed in the real conditions of your destination – you have stepped into an unfamiliar environment and must quickly learn to function effectively. You may feel a mix of trepidation and anticipation, anxiety and excitement. As you settle in, you will experience a period of adjustment to the conditions of your location. In this chapter we look at what it means to adjust and the impact it has on your attitude to your expedition. We then look at the notion of prioritising your needs as you colour in your maps, and describe activities that help you actively establish your ideal life.

Culture Shock – is it real?

In the current discourse on the experience of moving to live in a new country, the concept of 'culture shock' is commonly used to describe the experience of adjusting to a new environment. This theory of adjustment describes four main emotional stages (though variations on the theme add one or more phases): the honeymoon stage which is experienced as an exciting and positive period; the crisis stage during which typically frustration, anxiety and anger are felt; the stage of recovery in which the individual begins to come to terms with, and be able to function within, their environment; and the long-term adjustment or adaptation stage in which the individual once again functions normally and is satisfied with their life.

There are a few caveats to this model that we would like to point out. Firstly, the term implies that the process of adjusting is primarily about getting accustomed to a foreign *culture*. This is oversimplifying the matter. We identify three separate aspects of your experience that will require your adjustment.

- ➤ You need to adjust to the physical environment of your destination, (to *acclimatise*), such as the weather and the food. As you explore and adjust to your environment, you rebuild your physical map.
- ➤ You need to adjust to the local state of affairs created by the socio-economic and political organisation of society at your destination, (to *adapt*), such as the security situation, poverty/wealth levels and bureaucratic organisation. These aspects of your destination will primarily affect your activity map as you find ways to move unselfconsciously and with confidence through daily life.
- ➤ Finally, you will adjust to the culture and communication styles of the individuals you will meet and mix with (to *acculturate*). As you adjust to the way that you connect and communicate with others you will form the relationships that define your identity map.

We believe that it is vital to distinguish between these three adjustment processes. The first two, acclimatising your body and adapting your expectations to the reality of local life, are linked with the place that you have moved to and the new territory you are exploring (which we cover in this chapter). The third process, acculturation, is linked to the people, their culture, customs and ways of communicating (which we will cover in Chapter 7). Clearly this division is artificial and you will be adjusting to all aspects simultaneously. However, these are such big processes that we feel it is more useful to look at each separately.

The second caveat to the Culture Shock model is that it gives the impression that the phases described are inevitable: you will necessarily go through each one in sequence. However, recent studies of the emotional responses of people who relocate indicate that these emotional patterns are anything but inevitable or predictable. In the real experiences of international resettlers, some individuals do not experience the early period as an exciting, stress-free honeymoon but as difficult as pushing through pack ice. Other individuals state that they start in the honeymoon phase and remain there during their entire stay at their destination. Yet others find their adjustment to a new location a shock from beginning to end. Furthermore, moments of dissatisfaction or difficulty with one's destination can occur repeatedly over time, even many years into one's stay at any given destination. Therefore a 'one size fits all' model does not reflect the complexity of the individuals who are resettling abroad or the variety of situations that they are moving into.

We believe that it is more useful to look at the emotions you experience when adjusting as symptoms or outward expressions of your personal response to change rather than predictable defined stages of adaptation. In other words, it is better to look at adjusting as a process through personal change: we are all, in the end, individuals. We suggest that the emotions you experience depend on:

- Your expectation versus reality – the difference between what you *thought* you would find and the reality of what you find, and
- Your attitude to change – your *determination* to achieve your goal to resettle and create that ideal life for yourself.

The third caveat to the Culture Shock model is that the pre-defined curve gives the impression that you have little control over the emotional phases you experience: if you wait long enough, each phase will pass and you will eventually be happy at your destination. The philosophy of this book is that the knowledge, skills and attitudes of personal change management will help you gain control over how you experience the adventure of moving to live in a new country. You will go through emotional ups and downs – any good adventure has by definition moments that test your determination. But your happiness at your destination depends on the actions you take to create that good life for yourself.

So, instead of concentrating on the emotional process, let's look at the adjustment phases that cause these emotions.

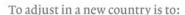

To adjust in a new country is to:
- Acclimatise to your physical location
- Adapt to the socio-economic and political conditions
- Acculturate to the people and their culture

How you feel during this process of adjusting depends on:
- How accurate your expectations were
- How determined you are to succeed

How successful you are at resettling depends on:
- The actions you take to adjust to your environment

Acclimatising

Within hours of your arrival, you are exposed to the environmental conditions at your destination. Your body will have to adjust to these new conditions: you may need to get over jetlag, or become accustomed to sleeping with or without air-conditioning or in a new bed; you may need to adjust to a new climate and to the different taste and quality of the food and water. This is the process of acclimatising.

It is easy to overlook the importance of this adjustment; much of it occurs subconsciously. However, your physiological adjustment process *will* have an impact on your well-being: adjusting costs energy. During this early period, you may be pushing yourself to accomplish as much as you can as quickly as possible. You need to expend more energy on everyday activities than you are accustomed to: activities which were effortless at home, for example going out to buy bread, can feel like an expedition in this new environment. How your body reacts to the change in your environment depends both on your physical make-up (for example, the resilience of your immune system) and the extent of the difference between your old and new environments. Whatever the factors, the strain of physiological adjustment increases your vulnerability to falling ill.

Your body's process of adjusting to its new environment can also affect your mental and emotional states. For example, if local food tastes radically different from that which you are accustomed to, you may begin to long for flavours you were accustomed to. Major changes to your diet, if you are ill or are over-tired and not sleeping well, can have a negative impact: the emotional consequences of acclimatising could be that you feel less happy about the move and your determination to succeed diminishes. In other words, the strain your body experiences as it adjusts to its new environment can lead to the sort of emotional reaction that corresponds to the 'shock' phase of the culture shock model.

Body Quotient (BQ)

Your BQ reflects what you know about your body, and how you deal with it. Do you listen to the signals it gives you or do you ignore them and just keep going? For instance, do you get enough sleep and do you eat food that gives or drains your energy? Your BQ affects how you function in your daily life because it affects how you feel, your state of mind, your self-confidence and your energy levels.

ADAPTED FROM JENSEN 2012

You cannot change local conditions. However, being aware of your body's acclimatisation process allows you to monitor how it affects both your energy levels and your attitude to your project to resettle. Understanding and managing your physical state is recognised as a form of intelligence: the Body Quotient. It is a skill, identifiable in top athletes and explorers that relates to your ability to know your body and to understand the impact the new environment has on you as well as your awareness of the actions needed to counter any negative impacts.

In the early stages of your move you can ensure that you get enough sleep, take vitamins to boost your immune system, or minimise the amount you try to accomplish in one day. You can try to get food you are accustomed to, prepare food that tastes like 'home', put a slice of lemon or orange in the water until you get used to the taste. Be patient with yourself and be proactive in finding ways to reduce the impact this physiological adjustment process has on your enthusiasm for your move.

Adapting

The conditions of your destination are more than just about the climate and geography: there are also the socio-economic and political conditions that have an impact on your daily life: a country's level of development, it's poverty and security situation all have an impact on the conditions you will experience. For example, government structures affect the efficiency of local bureaucracy and the quality and availability of newspapers, television stations, and telecommunication networks.

These are aspects of your destination that you probably became aware of during your research before arriving. However, it is very difficult to imagine what it will be like to live under certain conditions if you have never experienced them before. Though Shackleton knew the risks of Antarctic weather, he could not have prepared for the unusually harsh conditions that year. This reality is something he had to deal with when the voyage was already well underway. Once trapped in the ice, he had to adjust his plan and adapt to the situation.

As you rebuild your maps, you will probably discover that there are aspects of your environment that either do not live up to your expectations or that you simply had not expected to find. While some surprises may prove to be positive, some will invariably hinder your ability to achieve your mission. These could be small things that require minimal adjustment on your part or could be so large that they negatively impact your vision of success. For example, is traffic worse than you expected? Is the club that you had hoped to join now closed? Does the security situation restrict your movement more than you had anticipated?

When faced with such obstacles, one common reaction is to blame the location for the need to adjust: you can waste a lot of time and energy resisting reality, complaining about local conditions. The problem is that you cannot change what is. It may sound like a cliché but there is no other way of saying it: a place is what you make of it – it cannot make you happy or unhappy. Since you cannot change the conditions at your environment, you will need to somehow adjust your vision or activities, behaviour or expectations in a way that still allows you to create a good life for yourself at your destination.

Adaptation is difficult: it is not about becoming resigned to suffer for the length of your stay, but about dealing with frustration and loss of control to find solutions that work for you. It requires flexibility and determination, key skills both when resettling and in your career. How can you use the existing conditions at your destination to achieve your goal? Maintaining a problem solving, practical and pro-active approach to dealing with setbacks will allow you to move towards your goal of creating what you want.

Give yourself a long deadline for being settled, one year or more: you set yourself up for frustration and disappointment if you expect the process to be quick and easy. Keeping your long-term goals in focus even at this early stage is important. If you concentrate only on short-term settling-in goals you may forget to take actions that will pay off only later. For example, if you expect to stay at a destination for only a few years you may decide not to start the long-term strategy of learning the language as it will take too long before you can enjoy the results. But in the process of learning the language you could meet up with other newcomers with whom you share the journey of discovery. Attempting to learn the language earns you respect and recognition with the locals: this in itself is a good enough reason to take lessons. Taking a course may also give you a basis for a routine, stretch your mind to higher levels of Maslow's Hierarchy of Needs and give you a sense of achievement and pride in yourself. Finally, the result of long-range strategies such as learning the language is also beneficial if, like Shackleton for example, you suddenly find yourself staying for much longer than you thought.

Staying positive throughout the early process of adaptation is vital to your success: You must believe that with the effort you put into adjusting, you will, eventually, create the life you desire. It is human nature to allow a situation or event to colour your whole experience: one major hurdle at your destination can lead you to believe that you will never be happy. It would have been easy for Shackleton and his men to sink into despair when the *Endurance* froze within the ice flows. To dwell on the fact that they would never accomplish their original goal would not have helped the men in any way. Once they adapted their goal to that of getting out of Antarctica alive and well, Shackleton never allowed himself nor any of his men to ever doubt the eventual success of their mission. Shackleton's approach indicates a few ways to maintain your enthusiasm for your adventure:

- Be conscious of the good things: what do you enjoy; what are the benefits of your adventure?
- Keep everything in perspective: you may spend four years being frustrated by bad customer service, only to return 'home' and realise that the service is not as good at home as you had remembered.
- Keep your goal in perspective: how important is good customer service, really, to the quality of your daily life?
- Approach aspects of your new environment that you do not like as a 'to be dealt with' area rather than seeing such an aspect as impossible to change or a reason to give up and leave.

Taking control: planning and prioritising

It is easy to feel overwhelmed by the amount you need to accomplish in order to settle and create a new life. At this point you are faced with the challenge of rebuilding all three of your mental maps. Where to start with your planning and what your priorities are may seem difficult to identify. Useful research in this regard is work by Abraham Maslow on human motivation. Maslow looked at where highly successful people focused their time and attention in order to establish enjoyable, satisfying lives.

Maslow's Hierarchy of Needs (Maslow, 1970)

Maslow established an order or hierarchy of needs, indicating that people generally satisfy the needs at the base of the pyramid first: only when these needs are met do they turn their focus to fulfilling the next need higher up the pyramid. Of course, as you are working on rebuilding your three maps you will be looking to fulfil needs on all these levels. However, Maslow's hierarchy provides a useful structure for prioritising your list of things to do as you create that ideal life at your new location.

As an international resettler, you chose to move to a new environment to satisfy needs at the top of the pyramid – such as self-esteem, achievement and fulfilment needs – and may therefore be unprepared to find yourself in the first months dealing with needs at the bottom of the pyramid. These basic physiological needs, such as arranging housing, buying food, organising utilities, are survival-level needs. There are very few moments in life when individuals are required to satisfy these most basic of needs: crises, such as divorce or natural disasters, are examples of such moments. Focusing on this level of need can create a deep feeling of instability and insecurity, which can be an isolating experience if many people around you (including locals, colleagues, family and friends) have never relocated internationally, and are unaware of the emotional impact rebuilding your life can have.

Safety needs cover a wide range of concerns around personal and family safety caused by both the natural environment as well as the socio-political and economic conditions at your location. For instance, whether it is safe to walk the streets in the new neighbourhood, whether there are health risks such as malaria or poisonous insects and whether you have faith in the country's health services. It also includes elements of emotional safety such as feeling comfortable in dealing with local bureaucracy and feeling supported by the contacts you have locally as you set up your life within a foreign language or bureaucratic system.

Another source of insecurity is the fact that you do not yet have any daily or weekly routines: your work or school hours may be different, your weekly shopping, exercise and leisure schedules need to be established, and you don't know sufficient numbers of people to have a good social life. For a while, it may feel as if you are purely reacting to aspects of your destination, running from appointment to appointment, from place to place trying to accomplish your 'to do' list. This may give you the impression that you have lost control over your environment: your life can feel chaotic – you long for the order and routine of your former life, for stability, predictability and familiarity. Having the awareness that you are in the middle of a process of re-establishing your hierarchy of needs can bring a sense of control to what can seem to be an unstructured phase where priorities change quickly. Being aware that your experience is normal may help to give you the confidence you need to face the unknown and establish the life you want.

Some people experience the process of functioning in an unfamiliar environment as stimulating and gain energy from the challenge of discovery and the pay-off of learning something new every day. For others, the need to continually ask for information and not knowing how things work makes them long for the familiar. Remembering how effortless it was to go about their daily life 'back home' can leave them feeling tired, irritable or have a strong desire to wait at home until the place feels more familiar. Such feelings are part of what is called 'homesickness', which is a reaction to the emotional pressure of being in an unfamiliar environment twenty-four hours a day, seven days a week. Homesickness is an understandable and common response to the circumstance of change: it is OK to miss home. However, homesickness is about missing what you left behind rather than a reflection of your destination: recreating a satisfying life for yourself will help you fill the void of what you miss.

Colouring in your maps

Every step you take in mapping your new environment is a step towards establishing a sense of security and control for yourself. Breaking the process down into finite projects can help with this. A first step is the setting up of your home. Many people feel the need to have their 'nest' – not just a place to put suitcases – before they can venture out with confidence. For many, a full life begins once the container has arrived and been unpacked.

A next step is to establish a working knowledge of the basic facilities you may need in your environment. For example, you may want to learn where the health facilities are, their quality and level of service, and visit each one to register, meet a contact person and get phone numbers before you actually need them. This will increase your sense of security in dealing with unpredictable circumstances should you, or a member of your family, fall ill.

Find someone who can take you to places you need to visit. For this, you may need to learn to ask for help – the quicker you have established your physical and activity maps, the quicker you will be independent and self-confident in moving about within them. It could be useful to give yourself a daily task – today I will discover X – and then celebrate each achievement at the end of the day. You can divide your physical environment into concentric circles. You first discover the circle nearest your house, expanding to an outer circle when you feel you have mastered the first. Your goal here is to gain a sense of self-confidence in moving about your environment so that you can begin to create your vision of the life you wish to have.

In order to establish your routines, return to the activity map exercise in Chapter 3. What were the patterns in your daily/weekly and monthly life that you enjoyed? Looking at your vision of life, what are the routines and rhythms you need to establish in order to create that good life for yourself?

Establishing routines will involve doing things for *the first time*. You will need to negotiate unpredictable circumstances as you populate both your physical and activity maps. How do you get to work and what is the best route? Where is the grocery store and which will become your favourite? How much time does it take to get to places and what times are the worst for traffic?

Throughout this process, take time to note what you have accomplished and how much you have learned up to this point. A key part of leading oneself through change is the ability to look back and acknowledge how far you have come. Then, take a break from the necessity of establishing your life and do something fun – act like a tourist and explore an aspect of your location. Go to something that interests you like a fair, a museum, a film; walk around a particular historical or otherwise interesting area and just enjoy the place. Make more time to sleep or relax or do sports or take walks, whatever it is that allows you to not be 'settling in' but just to 'be'.

Adjusting as a family

Upon arrival, each family member will face similar stress factors. However, there are important differences in the conditions each individual faces in their personal adjustment process.

The accompanying partner

If you are a non-working partner in the family, you will have to create your entire new life structure – you will not have the benefit of falling into an established work or school environment. On top of that, you probably bear most of the responsibility for establishing the physical and activity maps of the other members of the family. It is the parent without the job that will most likely have the primary responsibility for discovering where the shops are, of setting up the home and establishing family routines, the children's afterschool activities and getting them to and from play dates. Many stay-at-home parents often concentrate on getting their children settled before they feel free to establish their own life. This delay in establishing your own routines may negatively affect how you feel about the resettling process.

Taking time to develop your own maps and satisfy your own pyramid of needs is important for two reasons. Firstly, if you are unhappy or feeling insecure or out of balance, you will be less able to fulfil the needs of the other members of your family. Secondly, children will take their cue from a parent who is a good role model on how to positively and actively establish a new life. Think of it like the emergency instructions in the airplane when you are asked to put on your own breathing mask first before helping your children: as counter-intuitive as this may seem, you cannot help others unless you are fully functioning yourself.

Children

On their first days at school, children will generally not be in the honeymoon phase. They may be frightened, intimidated by all the other children who seem to know where to go and what to do, overwhelmed and may be angry at you, their parents, for putting them in this situation. How each child experiences this new situation will depend on their personality, their age and developmental stage, and their individual approach to dealing with change, as well as their previous experiences with change (if any). Furthermore, how they express their emotions will vary too. Children may not express themselves verbally – they may change their sleeping or eating habits or become more clingy than usual. These signs may mean that they are reacting to their own stress or to emotional or behavioural changes they feel in you.

The conditions of your move will make a difference to the extent of adjustment your children will need to make. For example, children moving from one international school to another may find adapting easier. International schools are experienced in incorporating new students into their fold and making them feel at home. Local schools that have little or no experience in dealing with new or international children may not be aware of the range of difficulties children face in their adaptation process.

Another factor is how different the family structure is at this location compared to the last one. Have family customs changed, such as dinner times or who greets the kids after school? Are they now seeing less of a parent due to work commitments? Ideally, your home is a familiar and safe environment where there is open communication so that your children feel loved, understood and supported. Enabling children to communicate with family and friends in past locations and to talk about what they miss and what they have experienced allows them to express themselves and process their experiences.

As parents, there are many actions you can take to support your children's adjustment process. For example, talk to teachers and councillors at school, identify children that have some sort of similar background to your own and invite new friends over. For older children it is useful to allow them real choices in organising their lives: if the sport they want to do is not available, what is the next best option? Assist them in researching the possibilities and then support them in doing this activity. Remember, your children are building key change management skills– such as the skills of meeting new people and managing themselves through emotional reactions such as fear. They are developing strategies of what to do on their first day and first weeks in a new environment, skills that they will need time and again in their lives. You can help them understand that their emotions are reactions to change and that they can do things to reach the life they envisaged. The process of adjusting to change is not easy for anyone; they are not alone in their emotions.

The family

As each family member sets up their new routines and adjusts to life, there can also be relationship adjustments as roles within the family change. We spoke about this in Chapter 4, but now that it you are on location it is worth reviewing. The strain of individual adjustment combined with the adjustment of family relationships and dynamics can lead to stress or blow-outs. The bottom line in dealing with these family issues is that you are leaders in the process of change in the project of resettling abroad. Your attitude, reactions and actions will influence how those around you – your partner and children – will feel, act and react. If you are positive about the experience, take a problem-solving approach to dealing with issues and are determined to resettle successfully, then your family members will be reassured by your approach and learn from your example.

As a leader, it is important to acknowledge each individual's difficulties, to listen to their concerns and setbacks and to empathise with their feelings. There is often no space other than the family home where such emotions can be expressed. Finding concrete solutions to problems will show that you are truly interested in creating the conditions that will allow each individual to create that good life they have each imagined. The end question is:

are you truly enabling each individual in the family to create the life they want?

Characteristics of a mobile family

- The team has a shared goal:
  "We will resettle abroad"
- Team members take responsibility for success together:
  "We will make this work for everyone"
- The group has a team spirit:
  "We're in this together"
- Team members understand that success is a process:
  "It may not be perfect now, but we'll get there"
- Team members are open to learning:
  "We share our discoveries with each other"
- Team members are open to taking risks:
  "We try something new every day"
- Team members support each other:
  "We are available to help each other when the going gets tough"
- Team members have mutual respect:
  "Everyone's opinions are valid"
- Team members are open to each other's views:
  "We can discuss our differences"
- The team celebrates life and maintains humour:
  "Look at what we've achieved! Let's have a special dinner tonight"

The art of adjusting

There are several approaches that contribute positively to the process of resettling. These include being:

- Open to new experiences
- Determined to achieve your goals
- Optimistic in the face of challenges
- Flexible when looking at solutions to problems
- Tolerant of ambiguity and uncertainty

You and each member of your team will have a unique combination of the above. You do not have to love everything about your new location – no place is perfect: you do not always have to be in a good mood – expressing your frustrations and fears are a necessary part of dealing with them. However, your underlying attitudes to your destination and to dealing with change will affect your experience of the process – whether you enjoy the challenge of resettling in a new location or not.

Adjusting to your new life in a foreign environment is an art: adjusting involves the art of letting go of your past in order to fully enjoy your present. Your vision of your future is your guide – it is the framework that helps you take action, learn and make decisions. However, the art of international living is the ability to appreciate the present and not wait for the future to happen. This is the ability to stop and take time to appreciate the form your new life is taking. Such moments of delight can give you energy to tackle the rest of the day's *To Do* list: the view from your home or office window, the sound of rain on your new roof, the taste of a newly discovered fruit, the greeting from a newly made friend.

Adjusting to life in a new environment also results in personal development. People who adjust are more than what they were. To adjust does not mean that you need to 'give in' or alter what you think is important, but you can develop a new perspective without giving up who you were: you learn something new, do something differently, take up a new activity... always in the spirit of contributing to your end goal of creating your good life abroad.

In this chapter we focussed only on establishing your physical and activity maps through acclimatising and adapting to the conditions at your destination, and the planning and prioritising that will go with it. In the next chapter we discuss the processes of completing your identity map as you connect with and understand the culture of your new neighbours.

Optimism and unity on Shackleton's expedition

The crew of the *Endurance* included two groups of men: officers and scientists on one hand, and seamen on the other. In most expeditions of the time, these two groups were segregated, each with their own tasks and amenities. From the start of the expedition, Shackleton did away with the niceties of class and, though they slept in separate areas on the ship, he created one common living space and one set of rules for a united team. For men accustomed to the social hierarchy of pre-war England, this egalitarian system apparently took some getting used to.

> *I simply hate scrubbing. I am able to put aside pride of caste in most things but I must say that I think scrubbing floors is not fair work for people who have been brought up in refinement.*
> MARINE CAPTAIN THOMAS ORDE-LEES IN ALEXANDER 1998, P 17

For many months, and through the eternal darkness of Antarctic winter, the men found themselves in tight quarters with others they perceived as culturally different from themselves. Under Shackleton's leadership, they got down to the business of making the best of the situation. From the many diaries that survived, it is clear that there were some personality clashes compounded by class expectations of what constituted good behaviour. However, despite honest words put down on paper, everyone generally went about consciously trying to live as cordially with others as possible – conditions were already difficult enough, there was no need to make it worse by creating open discord among members of the team. Even in their private notes, men recognised those they disliked for their skills and talents, each for their contribution to the positive atmosphere in the group.

This camaraderie was in large part due to Shackleton himself who remained unflinchingly good humoured and optimistic throughout. As the leader, he took responsibility for exemplifying the positive attitudes he valued and participated in the social and work life on board.

> *To the credit side of the Expedition one can safely say that the comradeship and resource of the members of the Expedition was worthy of the highest traditions of Polar service; and it was a privilege to me to have had under my command men who, through dark days and the stress and strain of continuous danger, kept up their spirits and carried out their work regardless of themselves and heedless of the limelight.*
> SHACKLETON 1998, P 338

Faith in the intentions and capabilities of their fellow team members would prove vital with the onslaught of Arctic spring. Starting in August, the *Endurance* experienced grinding shockwaves from the shifting ice pack. In September the devastating power of shifting flows began to sap the confidence of the men on board that their ship could withstand the strain. In early October the ice under the ship melted and she floated in open water for several days. But then in the late afternoon of 18 October, the flows suddenly closed, pinching the *Endurance* sending her reeling to port. A few hours later the ice sheets parted and she righted herself again. For a few days the flows remained stable until, on 24 October the ice slammed into the ship again, this time cracking her hull. For three days the men fought tirelessly to save the *Endurance* from increasing attacks by the monstrous, heaving ice flows.

At 17:00 on 27 October, Shackleton said 'She's going boys. I think it's time to get off.' (Lansing 1999, p 60)

7 New neighbours

Sir Ernest Shackleton visited one of the few places on earth where no other human beings live. Wherever in the world your travels take you, you will need to not only live with the people who accompany you on your journey, but also get to know, and live among, the people who already inhabit the place. The contacts you make, the experiences you have with people and the friendships you develop will largely define the quality of your time at your destination. A party at the most impressive venue with the most sumptuous food and the greatest band will not be much fun if you are alone or do not meet interesting people. Like Shackleton's crew, the experience of your adventure will be more positive if you are surrounded by people on whom you can rely, and with whom you can grow, learn and have fun.

Let's return for a moment, to Maslow's hierarchy of needs to understand why your social contacts are so vital for your sense of well-being. Your initial contacts help you feel safe and stable in your new environment, fulfilling a part of your security needs: you need contact with people who acknowledge your existence and can help in case of ill health, babysitting or borrowing eggs when you run out. But once your basic needs are provided for, you address your social needs, for it is through your contacts that you build your identity and your sense of self-worth. Without a solid network of friends, colleagues, acquaintances and contacts you will not be able to create that ideal life you envisage for yourself.

Under normal circumstances, we build our social identity over a long period of time; it grows organically and quite subconsciously. However, when you move to a new location, the process needs to happen quickly. Your social network is so important to your success at your destination that it is worth taking time to consciously and deliberately build it up. Furthermore, even if you move from one city to another within the same country, you still need to establish your social network from scratch. However, if you are indeed resettling 'abroad' you are now in a foreign environment that brings an added complexity to the process: most of the people you meet are from a different culture: there is the culture of the local population as well as the culture of the organisation in which you work and the culture of the communities of other foreigners you may come into contact with. Adjusting to the culture(s) at your destination is what we call acculturation.

In this chapter, we will first look at the process of establishing your identity map – in whichever community you are. Then we add in the idea of culture and why it is an added complexity to your adjustment process. We look at four filters that influence how you react to another culture. Finally, we review approaches to effective acculturation.

Charting your identity map

Earlier in this book, you reflected on how your move would impact your identity: you thought of how you would want to see yourself as well as how you would want to be seen by others at your destination. The waypoints on this map are the:

- Roles in your professional life (boss/employee...)
- Relationships in your personal life (parent, friend, boss or house staff...)
- Status among friends, colleagues and other relations
- Memberships in various groups such as through the activities you do (a volleyball player, music fan...)

⋙ The way other people describe you (a leader, a sportsperson, ambitious, enthusiastic, a great friend, funny, knowledgeable…)

Like buildings on a street map, these people and relationships indicate where and how you belong in the social fabric of your destination.

How quickly or slowly you establish your identity map depends on both your personality and the conditions at your destination. How large your social network is and who is in it, depends largely on the type of individual you are. For example, do you tend to have an extensive group of contacts or do you prefer to have a few close friends? Where and how you meet people will depend on your lifestyle. Parents often make initial friendships on the school grounds; employees will make contacts at work. For others, it may require more effort and research to identify the people you want to make part of your network. If you are lucky you will know, or soon identify, at least one person who can initially introduce you to others. At your work you will quickly fall into your designated role and the work-related network linked to that role. But what about in your personal life? If you do not have a job, and you move with your partner who works at a large multinational accustomed to transferring staff internationally, you will probably have a certain amount of assistance and come into contact with a community of others who face the same challenges. If not, you may need to do all the legwork yourself, introducing yourself and building up a network of contacts.

One thing you may naturally do in the early stages of your arrival is to talk with friends and family back home. Because communication technology today makes it easy to keep very closely connected with 'back home', it is important you stay conscious of who you are spending most of your time and energy communicating with – local/new friends or people from home? However you build your network and who is in it, the point is that in order to achieve your ideal life you must consciously build it: what relationships do you need in order to create that good life you want to have? This process is so important to your goals that it should not be left to happenstance: but meeting people and building a social network is not necessarily easy.

An example of how your identity – both your own self-image and the self you see reflected by others – is affected during your first weeks and months at your destination is the fact that you are now the new kid in town. No one you meet has any idea of what you know, what you are good at, what you enjoy. They listen to you and watch what you do to learn about you. You must prove yourself every step of the way. As you navigate daily life among the new neighbours, you are 'foreign' in the most general sense of 'not from around here'. Everyone you meet is new to you, but to everyone else, you are the latest import, the stranger. Being in a new environment can, at first, make you feel dumb or incompetent: it is like joining in on a board game that you have never played before. You may normally be excellent at board games, but with this new one you are the only one who doesn't know the rules of the game, you make mistakes and continually have to ask for help. Some people are not too bothered by this experience; others feel uncomfortable and self-conscious.

Take a moment to consider how being new affects you. If you find it difficult, you may be inclined to limit your outings and delay the establishment of your network. One of the classic symptoms described in the culture shock model is the desire to sleep more than usual or to stay indoors and hibernate rather than going out to explore your new environment. Rather than being a reaction to a new culture, you may be reacting to the demands of constantly meeting new people regardless of their culture, being in an unknown social environment and always trying to guess the rules of the game.

The feeling of being new and out of your depth could be significantly greater if you move to a place with a different culture than if you move to a new city in the same country. Even if you transfer within an organisation, the new office will have a local culture that is different from what you are accustomed to. So what is, exactly, culture?

What is culture?

Your 'culture' is the set of values you hold that form the basis for your beliefs and attitudes. We generally use the term culture to refer to collective and shared sets of values: for example you can have your family, national or ethnic group culture. Culture is expressed in the way people behave – in what is considered good (or bad) behaviour and what is right and wrong. Another expression of culture is called 'high culture': the artistic expression within a society that includes the arts, festivals, celebrations etc.

Your culture is deeply subconscious: it is developed through the way you were raised by your family and through the influences of your teachers, friends and colleagues etc. Your culture is also 'personal': not everything you believe in comes from any given group culture – you share some values with people of your nationality but other values you developed from groups such as your family or from your personality and personal experience. In other words, you are not simply a representative of any given cultural group. For example, you may come from a society that values punctuality; agendas are planned, people are on time and dates are kept. You as an individual, however, may be considered 'chaotic' within your culture because you are often late, forget dates and prefer spontaneous activities.

The most commonly used analogy to visually define culture is the iceberg. The diagram below shows that observable behaviour – what you do and say – is only the very tip of what culture is. Everything below the waterline, your beliefs and attitudes developed from your deeper values are unseen and largely subconscious. However, it is upon these unseen and often unexamined elements that your behaviour is based. Because it develops subconsciously,

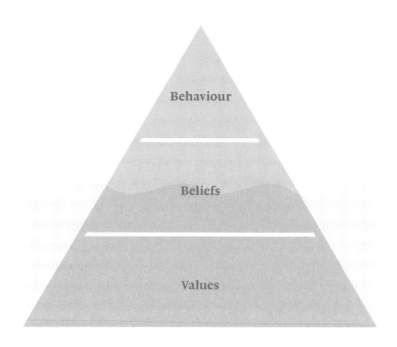

In 1976, Edward T Hall developed the iceberg analogy of culture in his book *Beyond Culture*

we humans are generally not aware of our 'culture' until we experience something different: children become aware of a different family culture, for example, when they sleep over at friends' homes where expectations of good behaviour may be different from what they know at home.

So what's the problem?

Why does encountering people with different cultural values create problems? There is no doubt that living and/or working in a different culture is a momentous process. An entire industry of cross-cultural communication and intercultural (both interpersonal and business) relations has sprung up in the last decades and hundreds of books have been written on the subject. Interculturalists (those who study cultural issues) divide cultures according to sets of values and give a range of behaviours that can express each value: for instance, how cultures regard time, whether they are hierarchical or egalitarian, or to what degree they are individualistic or group-based.

The challenge with 'culture' is the fact that it creates expectations and assumptions, most of which you are not consciously aware of. Remember, the basis for your culture are your deep-seated values – what you believe in, what you think is important, what you believe to be right and wrong in terms of attitudes and behaviours. When someone behaves in a way that does not 'fit' with what you believe to be proper, you could be shocked or confused or irritated: you can blame the other person for their behaviour.

In this chapter, instead of describing specific cultures or cultural traits you may encounter, we start from the idea that adjusting to different cultures is another aspect of managing yourself through change. There are many good books and training programmes that provide information on specific cultures and countries. We instead focus on the personal knowledge, skills and attitudes that you require to deal with any cultures that you may encounter. Adjusting to a different cultural environment is the process we call *acculturation*. To acculturate requires that you firstly understand your own values and the expectations and assumptions they create, and secondly that you identify the values, expectations and assumptions of members of the other culture. You do not need to take on another culture and abandon your own, nor is it useful to judge that culture as better or worse than your own – different is different, not better or worse. The point is that in order to establish that good life that you envisaged for yourself you will need to a) adjust your behaviour and communication patterns so that you are understood, listened to and accepted by those around you, and b) accept that there are aspects of the local culture that you cannot change. The goal is to create the life you envisaged with people you have chosen to bring into your network, whether they are from your own culture or other culture(s) at your destination.

To acculturate requires:

1 Knowledge of:
   a Your own culture
   b The other culture

2 The attitudes of:
   a Openness
   b Curiosity
   c Respect

3 The ability to:
   a Identify your impact on others
   b Adjust your behaviour and communication style
   c Accept difference

Filters

As you begin your life among new neighbours, building a social network that includes people of different cultures becomes complicated when you come across behaviours that you don't understand. How you interpret and react to the people and events around you is largely affected by what you *expect*. We have identified four key filters, or sets of expectations, through which you unconsciously interpret the behaviour of people from different cultures.

1 Your language filter

Your own culture has unspoken, unconscious, agreed rules of communicating. These rules act like a code for information you send and receive. The code can be seen as a filter for all the auditory and visual information you receive. Auditory information includes the words used as well as the way they are said: volume, emphasis, speed, variety of tone and number of pauses or interruptions you use. Visual information includes facial expressions and gestures/body language. This language filter is based on the expectations and assumptions you have of how people *should* communicate – what you expect to hear and see. When you communicate with people from your own culture, they use the same code and therefore it is easy to interpret what they are saying (easier – we still make mistakes even within our own culture). But when communicating with people from a different culture, you may communicate and decode messages using one filter but the other person communicates and decodes with another. For example, in some cultures, words are the most important element that contains meaning; in other cultures, the context of the communication greatly affects the meaning of the words spoken. Such contexts include who is involved in the communication (their relationship and status in relation to each other), who else is present during the exchange, what is said and *not* said and the way the words are delivered (in terms of body language, facial expression, tone). If you are only listening to the words, you may miss the real meaning of what is being implied through the context. If, for instance, someone is asked if they are coping with the experience of settling in to their new life, they may say 'yes, I'm fine,' but with their body language and within their cultural context they could be indicating that they actually would like more support: your language filter can stop you from understanding what other people really mean, and it can leave you frustrated when other people do not seem to understand you.

2 Your classification filter

Even before arriving at your destination, you developed an idea of what you expected the local culture to be like. As we described in Chapter 3, the information you base your vision of what it will be like to live among the people of your destination comes from a variety of sources including personal experience, television, books, the news, and what others have told you. Though it is important that you learn about and visualise the local culture, there is a danger that you formed a set of opinions about the local people that influence how you interpret them when you meet and deal with your new neighbours.

Cultures are hugely complex social constructs and the people within a culture are individuals, unique and multifaceted: and yet we humans tend to assign short labels and brief generalisations to 'others' that enable us to make sense of, and quickly reference, any given group of people. These automatic and simplistic mental pictures we hold about all members of a particular group are called generalisations or stereotypes. We use the word 'stereotype' here very carefully. A stereotype is nothing more than what we generally consider to be 'typical' of a certain group of people. We *all* have stereotypes: think of a rival city or town in your country. You will have a set impression in your mind – a short, punchy set of labels – about what 'they' are like and the behaviour you can expect when you go there. To give an example, we could say that the people of City A are industrious and hardworking but not very friendly. Logically, we are aware of the fact that our stereotypes are gross exaggerations: that the residents of City A are a lot of things beyond those few traits, and that not all residents, statistically speaking, will fit the label. Especially if you have been to that city, you realise that, though the stereotype may have a grain of truth since City A is a centre of business, the reality is that people of that city are much like those in your own city.

The problem with stereotypes is the subconscious attitudes they produce in people. Your generalisations about people in City A may simply be a short-form way of referring to the people of that city, as in 'people in City A *tend* to be like...' This type of generalisation or stereotype does not affect your attitude towards the people. At the other extreme, stereotypes can lead to prejudice where there is little room for alternative interpretation: 'people in City A *are*...' In this case, when you experience behaviour that confirms your assumptions and opinions you will think 'see, I knew it': but when you experience behaviour that does not conform to the stereotype, human beings tend to make exceptions for individuals but will maintain the belief in the general rule of thumb – what is actually your opinion or belief has now become a subconscious 'fact'. The stereotype is now the filter through which you view all people from that city.

Stereotypes, whether benign or prejudicial, act as a filter through which you interpret local behaviour. Because stereotypes are subconscious, they are not checked and re-evaluated. If you are unaware of your stereotypes and the behaviour expectations they form, you will interpret the slightest frown as unfriendly behaviour in City A. If, on the other hand, you are aware of your expectations and beliefs, you will be able to consciously test the truth of your opinions and come up with your own conclusions based on your firsthand experience. Take a moment to think about your opinions and expectations of the 'national' culture at your destination. Is there a difference between what you expected and the behaviour you are experiencing? Are you prepared to test the assumptions and opinions you have formed?

3 Your expectations filter

When you imagined yourself setting up your life at your destination, even though you tried to be as realistic as possible, it is likely that there were certain cultural behaviours that you were not aware of. You based your expectations on what you knew, planning your actions on social norms that you had already experienced. For example, a commonly experienced issue is that of meeting the neighbours. In some cultures a new neighbour is expected to introduce themselves to the established neighbourhood; in other cultures, established neighbours go to the newcomer's home to introduce themselves with offers of food and help with the move. In some cultures you will be interesting because you are new; in other cultures, people will be wary of you.

If you expect the neighbours to come around as you move in because that is good behaviour where you come from, and they don't, you might judge the locals to be cold and uncaring (forming a stereotype based on your experience). Then, when you are not invited to people's home for drinks or dinners, you may start to believe that no one is interested in you. This belief can lead you to conclude that you will never make friends at your destination. In other words, when reality does not match your expectations you form an opinion.

- Expectation   Neighbours will welcome me and I will build a community
- Reality   No-one has come to introduce themselves to me
- Opinions   I am alone and no one is interested in me
                 People here are not very friendly
                 I'll never make friends here

Forming such opinions is a normal process of learning from experience. The problem is that your initial expectation did not take the local reality into account – it was based on your own cultural values. The risk of forming your opinions about your host or other cultural groups early on in your stay is that this unconscious process of forming opinions is often not based on an accurate understanding of the reasons for the behaviour you witness. Misunderstanding behaviour can lead to disappointment, which leads to negative opinions. In the example above, while you think your neighbours are cold and unfriendly, they think that the foreigner who has come to live among them seems uninterested in getting to know them. Perhaps all it would have taken is to ask what good neighbourly manners look like. Had you knocked on the door of one or two homes, a completely different experience would have resulted, leaving you with a different opinion of and behaviour towards your neighbours and they with a different opinion of and behaviour towards you.

The problem with the opinions you form is not just that they may not be accurate, but more importantly for you as a resettler, that they may limit the actions you take to develop your network, thereby blocking you from achieving your goal of creating a good life for yourself. If, to continue with the example above, you believe that you will never make friends with the local neighbours, you may not get to know some of the people who are key to your goal. You may give up on achieving that ideal life because conditions are, according to you, not favourable. Behaviour that strikes you as odd or 'wrong' stems from a value that is different to your own. Understanding the cultural reasoning behind the reality you experience will allow you to reconsider the opinions you have formed through your expectations filter in another light. Remember, you may feel uncomfortable with certain behaviour but another person from your same cultural background may not even notice it, or may even find it endearing. How you feel about the culture you witness is as much about you as it is about them.

4 Your identity filter

The way in which local people react to you can affect your self-image. For example, in some cultures you may be respected and have status simply because of the title you have, or the knowledge you bring: in other cultures you may have to earn respect through your actions and local achievements. Your past achievements are often an important part of your identity and sense of self-worth;

if they are not recognised, you can feel as though you lost a part of what makes you, you. On the contrary, you may be given status at your destination purely based on your title – or your partner's title – which, while flattering, can be confusing. High status can mean that others expect certain behaviour of you. For example, the 'boss' may be expected to care for his staff outside of the office in terms of entertaining and solving their personal issues: you may be the boss or the boss's partner on weekends as well as during the week. Were you prepared for this role that came with your title?

Shackleton's crew had to deal with issues of status among themselves, status related to their jobs on the expedition but also to their positions in British society. In the same sense, you need to be aware of your own attitude to status. Are you meeting people from the local culture that have a similar education and socio-economic standing to you or are you primarily meeting subordinates at work or people in a service position (such as shop keepers, restaurant or household staff)? If you subconsciously feel a difference in status, this can create a feeling of distance between you and others in which you may feel disconnected from or even superior to the local culture. You may find it hard to gain trust, respect or good will from a position of superiority.

Acculturation

There are aspects of the culture at your destination that you cannot change: some you like and some go against your basic values and make you feel uncomfortable. Once you understand the concept of culture and the filters through which you evaluate and interact with other cultures (and through which they evaluate and interact with you), you can identify ways of coping with differences so that you can build the quality of life you desire.

This coping process, or acculturation, is to adjust to the local culture in such a way that you can achieve your goal. To acculturate means that you make an effort to understand and be understood by your new neighbours. This might sound irritating – you are new and overwhelmed with acclimatising and adapting AND you have to make an effort with the neighbours when it would be so much easier for them to make the effort to understand you instead. Well, true – but your hosts cannot be asked to adjust to your way of doing things. You will need to come to terms with the fact that the behaviour you witness is equally acceptable to the people of that culture as your behaviour is to you – you don't need to adopt this behaviour yourself, but you do need to respect the fact that this is how things are done in your new environment. There will be aspects you don't like. Therefore, to help yourself, you may need to understand the reasons behind them – the norms, values, beliefs and traditions that have shaped the behaviour – and then find a way to best deal with it. Here are a few ways of consciously undertaking this process.

1 *Choose who you know*

As you set out to populate your identity map, it is natural to seek out people 'like yourself', people with whom you have something in common. The most obvious similarity is people of your own nationality, culture or language background. With these people there is less guessing about the rules of the game; it is a safe and familiar environment. Many people in many locations find it much easier to quickly settle in and be effective in daily life if they limit their physical surroundings and activities to international circles. In some locations where people live in enclosed compounds, there are few other options. So, because of the difficulties in functioning within a foreign culture you may be tempted to restrict your network to people of your same cultural background. However, in your vision of your ideal life abroad, to what extent do you intend to stay separate within the foreign community or among people from your own cultural group?

Here are three factors to consider:

- ⟫ Remaining in the 'expat bubble' limits your experience of the culture, colour and flavour of your specific destination;

- ⟫ Experience shows that those who choose to limit their contact with the local society are more likely to develop a 'them and us' attitude. A lack of knowledge and understanding of the filters of the local culture can lead to misunderstandings and irritation. This experience will definitely detract from the enjoyment and satisfaction of living at your destination;

- ⟫ Though initially it may be more complex and challenging to get involved in local society, experience proves that you will undoubtedly grow from the experience and be rewarded for the effort you put in. Contact with the local culture will build your intercultural communication skills and your ability to understand and value different cultural viewpoints, behaviours and customs.

Who you choose to include in your network will be impacted by your personal situation and local conditions such as:

- ⟫ How long you intend to stay
- ⟫ How open you are to living within a foreign culture
- ⟫ How open the local culture is to accepting foreigners
- ⟫ Whether you will actually have access to the local community

So, what sort of people do you need to have in your network in order to achieve that ideal life you envisage? For example, you may wish to meet people (regardless of their culture) who:

- share a similar interest – like a sport, hobby or job
- have similar educational or socio-economic background or upbringing
- have similar life experiences, such as international travel, or having small children or older children that are not with you...

If you are having difficulty dealing with the local culture, you may be able to find others with whom to share your frustrations. While the company of such people may feel comforting for a while, be wary of the fact that together you may become 'complaint buddies'. Are your current contacts helping you take the steps you need to achieve your goal, or are you mainly just agreeing together that your life is not what you had hoped it would be?

There are two types of individuals who can be particularly helpful in dealing with cross-cultural relations:

- 'Bridge people' are individuals either of your own nationality who have typically lived in your host culture for years and have developed a respect for and understanding of the culture, or they are from the host culture but have lived abroad in a country similar to yours. Such individuals are often able to explain the differences between local customs and norms and your own cultural expectations because they have a deep understanding of the values and beliefs that underlie both.
- 'Code breakers' are people who are naturally aware of language and behaviour filters and communication codes. These can be the children of mixed-culture marriages or people who were otherwise raised in a multicultural community, serial expats or people who lived in different countries as children. Whatever their personal circumstances, these people tend to look for meaning beyond words when they communicate with people of a different

culture. Even if they do not know the host culture, code breakers will help you reflect on expressions or behaviours you do not understand in the local community.

The point of meeting these people is that they are generally positive about the country and culture you live in. They will be able to help you explore your new territory by explaining, from your cultural perspective, the behaviour you witness, because they understand the values, norms and beliefs that underlie the culture. For example, you can make a list of 'things I don't understand' on which you put everything that you find bewildering, incomprehensible or irritating. Then ask a bridge person or code breaker about it. They can help you decipher the context that makes this behaviour appropriate/ understandable.

Meeting people who have built successful lives at your destination can be inspiring and can open doors you may not have thought of. And these people can help you meet locals with whom you have common interests. The more people you meet from the local culture, the less you will fall into the 'them and us' trap that can isolate you from locals and limit your opportunities for establishing your ideal life.

2 Adjust your filters
Your ability to communicate with people from different cultures requires that you take into account their perspective (frame of reference or point of view) in interpreting the messages they send you. It depends on your openness to accepting that your code is not what is 'right' but that it is your way of doing things. To give people the benefit of the doubt and to be open to difference depends on your ability to empathise with the point of view of others and your desire to understand the subconscious framework that the other is working within. This requires a certain amount of self-confidence – you must feel comfortable in maintaining your own values and beliefs while acknowledging the fact that there is another point of

Moral Quotient (MQ)

MQ relates to your personal integrity, your sense of responsibility, your ability to empathise with other points of view and to forgive yourself and others. People with high MQ are honest, keep the commitments they make to themselves and to others and maintain their integrity even when under stress.

ADAPTED FROM JENSEN 2012

view. People who experience different cultures from an early age often have an instinctive understanding that their code is only one of many codes, that other ways of doing things may not be their preferred approach but is equally valid.

Each individual has a natural approach to others; we are all, to various degrees, empathetic, though some people are more attuned and open to the perspectives and feelings of others. Our levels of empathy can vary according to whether we are dealing with family, people we know, strangers or people from different cultures – we tend to be most empathetic towards those who are closest to us. Empathy is an element of what is known as Moral Intelligence (MQ). Your level of personal integrity and self-confidence, combined with empathy and honesty towards others determine your MQ and thus your ability to deal with living in different cultures.

3 Explore

The more you learn about the culture of your new neighbours, the easier it will be to establish your identity map and achieve your ideal life. To do this you can read books or obtain training on the culture. Read the local papers to get a sense of what is going on the country and what people are talking about, what preoccupies them, what issues and daily difficulties do they have, what hopes and aspirations do they have for their country/people.

Mingle. Talk about your culture and theirs and look for similarities. A lot is made of our differences, but there are more similarities than there are differences between cultures. Share stories, anecdotes, traditions and expectations. In other words, you can approach 'culture' as an anthropologist – as an adventure, a trip through discovery of how and why other people do things.

Attitudes that make it easier to deal with foreign cultures:
- Openness
- Humility
- Humour
- Open-mindedness
- Flexibility
- Willingness to compromise
- Desire to learn and experience adventure
- Curiosity about other people/other cultures
- Ability to cope with ambiguity
- Self-awareness
- Being open to personal change/growth
- A solid sense of personal identity that is not threatened by differences

Learning and growing

Adjusting to life in a new country involves acculturating to a new culture, forcing us to examine our own values, beliefs, norms and expectations. The process requires us to call up and use skills and attitudes we may otherwise have never used, increasing our resourcefulness and self-reliance. Adjustment requires self-reflection and analysis, which can be uncomfortable, and therefore some people try to avoid it. However, in order to adjust to living among people of another culture, you must consciously learn about your own culture as well as the culture(s) of those around you. You need to develop the ability to question your own assumptions and be open-minded and empathetic towards others as you populate your social network and develop your identity map. The process will be easier if you remain positive and determined to achieve your vision of a good life. After a while, you will begin to realise that your new life is taking shape and you can settle into ensuring your success over the duration of your stay.

Shackleton's crew make a life on the ice

Shackleton was aware of the emotional impact being 'homeless' would have on his men. So he decided that rather than sit and wait, they would trek across the ice to open water. Using the dogs and their own strength, they pulled the heavy wooden lifeboats containing their remaining possessions. But crossing the jagged, ever-shifting ice took too much energy: after three exhausting days they established Ocean Camp. On 21 November, from a distance of 1.5 miles (2.4 km), they watched the final agony of the *Endurance* as she was swallowed by the cold Antarctic sea.

But in the warmer spring weather, the ice pack slowly rotted, making camp life wet and precarious. On 23 December the team packed up again, glad to have a plan and be in action. After six days of toil, Shackleton ordered the establishment of Patience Camp on a solid-seeming patch of ice. For three and half months they lived in their tented community, practiced emergency evacuations, and established night duty.

Shackleton kept constant tabs on the mental and physical state of his men. The good news was that they were drifting north across the Antarctic Circle. They got to within 60 nautical miles off Paulet Island but the pack was too loose to allow them to walk to it and too tightly packed for them to sail in the boats. On 7 April they observed Clarence Island. They were so close to open sea that they felt the ocean swell, 28 men perched precariously on their 'floating cake of ice' (Shackleton 1998, p 120), surrounded by marauding killer whales and careening icebergs. Finally, on 9 April, seeing veins of open water, Shackleton ordered everyone and as much material as possible into the three lifeboats. For four days the pack protected them from the worst of the sea's wind and swell, but eventually they made a two-day non-stop dash across the open sea. They ran out of water, could barely rest, and struggled to keep the three boats afloat and in sight of each. Finally, drenched and exhausted, they landed on the rocky, barren shore of Elephant Island.

Shackleton calculated that they had food reserves for three months on reduced rations: it was clear that he would need to go in search of help. On 24 April, he and five volunteers set sail for South Georgia Island in the 22 -foot (6.9 m) lifeboat, *James Caird*. For 17 days and nights they fought to stay alive, bobbing wildly on the roughest body of water in the world. Both men and boat were already weakened physically: with the bare minimum of protective clothing and little food and water, they suffered frostbite, gale force winds and the largest wave Shackleton had ever witnessed. Their approach to the island was nearly fatal because of treacherous reefs, glaciers and sheer rock cliffs towering 100 feet (30 meters) above the shore.

Shackleton's story is one of sheer determination, setting one foot after the next on the only logical course possible – towards safety. He never questioned whether he would succeed. As he struggled to reach help, another story was unfolding – that of the men left on South Georgia Island who saw the small lifeboat fight its way into impossibly stormy seas. Frank Wild was left in charge of the remaining men with orders to make for Deception Island if help did not arrive. They couldn't know if Shackleton would survive the crossing. But Wild never let them doubt that sometime in August they would be rescued...

8 Settle down

After several months at your destination, life starts to take shape. The busy chaos of setting up your home, getting to know people and understanding your surroundings subsides as your daily life takes on routine and structure; you can finally start to relax. At this point, some people experience a strange feeling of emptiness. This generally occurs when you have, for the most part, settled in your new environment – your physical, activity and identity maps, though not complete, are detailed enough to allow you to function 'normally' on a daily basis. The adrenaline of the initial stress has worn off; time is no longer full of urgent things to do; the emotional highs and lows flatten out leaving you with time and emotional space to reflect on your current life. This may be the moment when you fully realise the finality of your situation: this is not a short-term holiday – this is IT. This is the location you have chosen, the place where you will live for the foreseeable future. For some people, the reality of their destination stretching before them in an endless sea of time is enough to make them want to abandon ship. In other words, at this junction in your stay you may be asking yourself, so what now?

This is the point at which the vision of your good life becomes important. How close is the life you are currently living to the goal you created for yourself before leaving? You may be coming along quite well, or there may still be hurdles you need to overcome to reach your goals. In the chaos of settling down you may have you gotten sidetracked down a path you had not planned, that you didn't consciously choose or that is not part of your original vision but which developed as a result of the people you met and the activities you chose in the beginning. Now that your basic needs are taken care of, you can focus on your long-term goals, on establishing that good life for the duration of your stay at your destination.

Long-term strategies

Whether you intend to stay at your destination only for a few years or for a lifetime, there is a difference between having the intention to merely survive the experience or being committed to living a full life for the duration of your stay. We believe that the monumental effort of moving from your established home to a new destination is not worth it if you are not committed to making the best life possible for yourself at your destination. Once the initial stage of resettling is over, we have identified five strategies that help you focus on your long-term commitment to achieving your ideal life.

1 Keep perspective

Even after an initially successful period of getting settled, you may reach a stage where everything seems wrong or the things you don't like take on such proportions that you can see nothing else. Your ability to keep the big picture in mind is vital at this point. Shackleton had the knack of keeping sight of the bigger picture: once it was clear that his ship was stuck in ice and that his original destination was out of reach, he put all his energy and skills into getting every one of his men home.

For the international resettler, your 'big picture' is that ideal life you planned for yourself. What did you hope to achieve at your destination: remember back to when you were deciding whether or not to actually move, how did you foresee that this destination would contribute to your life's aspirations? When you look out at the horizon, can you see past the details of what is not right and glimpse what would remain unlived or unachieved if you were to return home today? Take a step back from the microscope through which you view your daily experiences. That thing that annoys you, is it really that important in the bigger picture of your ideal life? Place the aspects that bother you on a mental 'to be dealt with' list rather than on a 'this is unsolvable' list. This makes it easier to come up with steps you can take to cope with the aspects of your destination that affect your satisfaction with your daily life. Taking a step back to view the broader picture also reveals the enjoyable aspects that your destination does have to offer.

2 Choose the positive

It is human nature to judge or remember an experience by the bad things that happen – you are in a hotel for one week and even if everything else goes well, one bad experience can colour your whole memory of the holiday. Especially if things go wrong in the beginning, setbacks you had not anticipated can make it very difficult for you to maintain your enthusiasm for your adventure. Though there are aspects of your environment you cannot change, you have control over how they affect you and how you deal with them as you create your good life. How you deal with the process of adaptation has a lot to do with your attitude to firstly, the process of change and secondly, to your location. The men that Shackleton left behind on the rocky outcrop in the middle of the Antarctic sea could only wait to be rescued. But they still had choices in how they dealt with the situation: they could give in to despair or take their fears out on each other, or they could choose to make the best of a terrible situation. You have gone through a long process of upheaval to get where you are today – the choices you made in the past led you to this place in time. You are now grappling with the consequences of your decisions. In this sense, if you are having trouble committing to the idea of staying at your destination, you may be getting in the way of your own happiness through your attitude to your experience. Your destination cannot make you happy – only you can choose to take the necessary steps to become happy. Therefore, your attitude towards your destination will greatly affect your long-term ability to create that good life for yourself.

3 Be realistic

If you are looking at your past location through a telescope, you may have a tendency to idealise your life there to the detriment of life at your new destination. Among people who move from posting to posting, there is the phenomenon known as 'serial disenchantment' or 'the grass is greener in the past' in which an individual claims always to have been happiest at their last posting. In this sense, it is easy to compare the last period at a location, when you were entirely settled, with the first period at a new destination when life is still so 'unsettled'. You can gain a more realistic perspective by making an effort to consciously add to this comparison the good aspects of your current location, the things you enjoy, as well as the aspects of your last location that you did not enjoy.

4 Manage change consciously

Feeling high levels of irritation regarding your new environment can be a sign that you are resisting change. We discussed approaches to change in Chapter 3, but now that you are in the middle of the experience, look back at how you thought you would react and how you are now really reacting to change. To adapt to your environment means that you will undergo change: you will learn new things, do things differently and see things in a new light. But change is not easy. Are you still holding on to aspects of your past life that make it difficult to embrace your new environment? You may, for example, still be spending more time talking to people at your old location than at the new one. Are you focussed on your next holiday away rather than on building your current life? Self-awareness regarding your approach to change gives you control over how you experience adjustment – the 'problem' isn't your environment: the problem is how it makes you feel. You may have gotten yourself into a vicious circle with the wait-and-see approach, subconsciously waiting for your new life to fall together and for you to be happy. If this is the case, you may not have proactively developed the kind of network, activities and routines you want in your life, which may feel like further evidence that you made a wrong choice in your new destination. Look at what you can do to adjust your approach to change and start to do things differently. For example, are you taking full advantage of the opportunities available at your destination? In order to do so, you may need to, if you haven't already done so, acquire the skills appropriate to your environment such as learning the language, taking driving lessons that allow you to better deal with local driving habits, or any skill that helps you adjust to local conditions.

5 Be aware of the adaptation process over time

Difficult moments can happen at any time during your adventure – even years into your new life. Adaptation is not something that happens once and is finished. It continues, incrementally, even if you live in a foreign country the rest of your life. The longer you live in a place, the more you learn about it and the more you discover subtle differences with your own culture or socio-economic conditions. Friendly curiosity can turn to cynicism and disdain as you reject some aspects of your environment. The point to remember is that you do not need to love everything about your environment but you must accommodate it. To this end, you may need to fight for and persevere in developing an aspect of your life that can make the difference between thriving in your location, or just surviving your experience.

Vulnerable moments

Clearly, life is a cycle; it is never static. At any given moment in your adventure you may encounter vulnerable moments that threaten your commitment to stay at your destination.

Within your first year(s) at your destination, there are certain moments or events that can affect your attitude towards your adventure. For example, the experience of returning 'home' for the first time – for holidays such as Christmas or Saleh, or home leave – can create a vulnerable moment in your determination to create a new life for yourself for several reasons. Firstly, it affects your sense of belonging at 'home'. On the one hand, it is a great feeling to be back in a familiar environment, to have a break from settling in. Or, it can be unsettling: you may realise that the 'home' crowd cannot understand the impact of moving to a new country and of adapting to a new culture. They may seem only superficially interested in your experiences abroad, unable to imagine themselves in the same position and therefore cannot empathise with you. This may leave you feeling isolated and misunderstood when you expected sympathy. Also, your old environment may no longer feel like 'home' since you no longer have a place in people's daily lives. This experience can be positive because it helps you realise that home is not what (or where) it used to be, allowing you to take an emotional step away from your past. On the other hand, realising that you no longer belong as you once did may feel like a loss.

Secondly, a holiday can also affect your sense of belonging at your new destination: upon your return you may feel relieved to be back. This maybe the first time you experience your new location as 'home'. This is a major landmark as you begin to see yourself as belonging, returning to a familiar environment and realising that your new house has become home. It is a similar experience at work where you may remain 'the new person' until another person joins your team and then overnight you realise you have become part of the 'old' crowd. On returning 'home' you become aware of just how much you have built and achieved in your new life, the routines, the friends and the sense of purpose you have. On the other hand, the return after a holiday away can feel like a plunge back into the chaos and ups and downs of adaptation. You can take more control of this experience by consciously reviewing your successes since moving to your destination, to take stock of what you have achieved and what you have left to do.

Vulnerable moments can occur when something changes in your family environment, such as the death of someone very close, the ageing of parents, or the 'empty nest syndrome' when children leave home. These are major life-events under any circumstances but are compounded in complexity and emotion by the fact that you live in a foreign environment. For example, if you don't return to your family for important yearly milestones like birthdays or graduations, you may feel guilty about not being there and feel you are missing out on what is happening in their lives.

The decisions you take as a result of these vulnerable moments will depend on your own circumstances, but also on your commitment to your adventure. If you adopted the 'wait and see' strategy described in Chapter 3, any one of these vulnerable moments may be the trigger that tips you to the point where you feel that you have reason enough to leave. Given the huge amount of energy and effort it has taken you to get this far, it is important to identify whether the reason you want to leave is the impact of a vulnerable moment, or whether the situation itself, or new factors are the reason. For example, a divorce, a natural disaster or a serious illness of one of your family members may leave you with no choice but to leave in order to get to the best place and situation you need to be in order to deal with your current situation. The point here is that the decision to abandon your project should not be made within the emotional context of a vulnerable moment. The decision to review your choice to move should not be a move away from the difficulties of resettling at your destination, but rather be a move towards the best solution given your current circumstances.

Raising mobile children

One specific situation that affects people in their decisions regarding the mobile life is the idea of raising international children. One of the concerns of mobile parents is the idea of not providing their children with roots. Particularly parents who themselves grew up in one stable location can feel guilty that they are not giving their children the familiar and trusted upbringing that they themselves received. What you did as a child feels 'right' to you: you will value your experiences and the idea of growing up in a fixed environment. Raising your children in an unknown and ever-changing environment may make you question whether you are doing the right thing for your children.

In order to address the issues of what your children may or may not miss out on, it is useful to review three aspects of what is, often subconsciously, meant by the term 'roots'. Firstly, people often mean a 'national identity'. It is true that your 'home country' may not feel like home to your children, especially if they cannot remember ever living there. When mobile individuals are asked by non-mobile people 'where are you from?', they expect a straightforward answer – we live in a world divided into nation states in which individuals are given rights (such as a birth certificate and therefore legitimacy) and responsibilities (like loyalty and paying taxes) based on their nationality. Your children will most likely have a passport from your country but may not identify with it.

This brings us to the second aspect of the notion of 'roots': culture. How your children experience the issue of 'where they are from' depends on your ability to give your kids a sense of being grounded in a culture (or several cultures) and a family, regardless of the place you live, and of helping them deal with questions from non-mobile family and friends who don't understand the benefits and complexities of their lives. Think of the aspects of your childhood or of the non-mobile lifestyle that you think your children may miss out on. Can you provide those in other ways? For example, familiarity with customs and traditions from home can be provided during extended holidays with family, summer camps, and experiences where they learn about their 'roots'. Also, take note of the things that your children will gain from the mobile life: the skills and knowledge and attitudes that are useful for the globalised world of the future such as languages, flexibility, multicultural skills and self-reliance.

A third way of looking at roots is in the formation of close and permanent social ties. The mobile life means that children do not grow up surrounded by a stable community of people like those children who grow up in the same neighbourhood. For this reason, it is vital that their immediate family – you, their parents as well as their siblings – provide all the support and stability they need. Mobility can mean that children repeatedly say goodbye to old friends and need to make new ones. Technology today means that children can maintain contacts internationally far easier than previous generations could, and they develop skills in meeting new people and quickly making intense friendships that can be maintained over distance and time. Again, you as a parent play an important role in how your children experience the process of creating lasting relationships: you set an example by creating solid family ties and supporting your children to maintain good family relationships and helping them keep up their friends around the globe.

Overall, non-mobile people tend to see 'roots' as something that is grounded in a specific location, like the roots of trees. To mobile children, 'roots' are grounded in the culture of their family and friends, in their experiences in the places they lived and in the strength of their own values and beliefs that you give them through your upbringing. Their roots are more like the portable roots of orchids than the fixed roots of trees.

Whether the experience of the international lifestyle is positive and 'normal' for your children will depend, not on anything 'inherent' in the mobile life itself, but on the role you play in guiding them through the issues of resettling abroad. Children will quickly establish their physical, activity and identity maps through school, clubs and hobbies. However, they will need your leadership and guidance in understanding the processes they go through and recognising the skills, attitudes and knowledge that they gain along the way.

One example is how your children benefit from, and deal with, people from different cultures. Children quickly pick up on cues about how to behave towards 'others' through their family and surroundings. Be aware that your children will pick up on your words, body language, stereotypes and judgemental opinions; your negativity about the local culture will be taken by them as a cue to feel the same way. In an international move, you want your children to be happy and well adjusted, which means that they need to develop empathy and respect for people from other cultures. Being a good role model in this will be vital, as will talking about any negative judgements and stereotypes that they express. Again, this is not to say that you must love everything about any given culture: dislikes can be expressed and discussed but so should positive aspects. An international move is an opportunity for your children to grow into responsible international citizens who can be comfortable in any social situation.

There are pros and cons to both the non-mobile and the mobile styles of life: both are viable options; neither path is wrong. On the planet today, many more people lead their life within one country than those who move between countries. However, the world is getting smaller and a growing number of people are from mixed cultural backgrounds, mobile or immigrant families – all of whom have an allegiance to or heritage from more than one nation. In deciding between the two lifestyles, you need to decide what is best for your family, taking into account your family circumstances, the conditions of your move, and the personality and needs of each individual involved.

For example, unilingual parents who struggle to learn a second language worry about raising their children with more than one language. All research on this matter points toward the positive effects of bi- or multilingualism on the cognitive abilities of children. Languages are skills that will give them an edge on the job market in the future, and open their minds to learning more languages should they ever want to in the future. Are your worries about your children's language learning coming from your adult perspective rather than from your child's abilities and interests?

Raising children in the culture of one partner brings with it specific issues that must be talked through. The 'foreign' parent may want to spend time with their children in their own cultural environment in order to give their cultural history and background to the children. Even if the children themselves live their whole lives in only one country and just visited the other one, they will be more than just a national of the country they live in – they will have cultural influences from somewhere else and may well identify themselves to some degree with that other culture. Children are, from a very early age, aware of language and cultural differences – they know, for instance, that they can tell certain types of jokes with one set of grandparents but not with the other; that they speak one language in one family context and change the style of communication as well as the language they use in another family context. These skills in cultural empathy, awareness and flexibility are advantages they develop naturally from their international background.

Ensuring that your children benefit from your mobile lifestyle is a long-term project. You will need to guide them through the strategies and vulnerable moments mentioned above. To this end, following yearly rituals is important – birthdays, religious festivities – whatever is 'normal' in your year. Celebrating these events helps the new destination feel like home. Adding a touch of local flavour to each routine will help cement the old ways of life to the new. Celebrating Christmas in the tropics when you are used to snow is exotic: so is celebrating Saleh in the snow when you are used to the heat and sunshine.

Settled in

The mobile life is a choice you and your family make consciously and create together. Your ability to focus on your goal will help you commit to the long-term implications of settling at your destination. In this chapter we looked at the mindset and skills required to successfully relocate over time. In terms of knowledge, you need to be aware of your approach and emotional responses to the adaptation process as well as the impact that both the mobile and non-mobile lifestyles have on your children. Your attitude to both your destination and to the process of change will impact not only your experience, but that of your children as well. Remaining positive and curious about your destination will help you deal with the strain of personal change. In terms of skills, your ability to focus on and work positively towards your goal as well as maintaining perspective on your experience will ease the process. Your ability to accept and deal with the consequences of your decision will help both you and your children through the long-term adaptation process.

The end of Shackleton's expedition

On 10 May, Shackleton and his five crewmembers landed on the wild and uninhabited southwest coast of Georgia Island: the whaling station lay to the extreme east of the Island. They rested for a few days to recover but Shackleton was eager to press on. On 19 May, Shackleton and the two fittest men set off on foot to cross the uncharted island. They had a sketchy map, three days of food rations each, one Primus lamp with enough oil for six hot meals, a small cooker, one carpenter's adze for use as an ice axe, 50 feet (15.24 m) of rope and 48 matches. They walked, climbed, slid and dangled through a waterfall and dared not sleep for fear of freezing to death. After 36 hours they arrived at the station they had left 1.5 years earlier with nothing but the clothes they had been wearing for a year, the adze, logbook and cooker.

> *...but in memories we were rich. We had pierced the veneer of outside things. We had "suffered, starved, and triumphed, grovelled down yet grasped at glory, grown bigger in the bigness of the whole" ... We had reached the naked soul of man.*
> SHACKLETON 1998, P 205

Even before he had a single night's sleep, Shackleton spent every minute, using his significant network and reputation to arrange a rescue of the men on Elephant Island. Three days after his arrival, Shackleton left on an English boat; they got to 100 nautical miles of the men, but were stopped by impenetrable ice. On 10 June they tried again, this time on a Uruguayan-loaned ship. They got to within sight of the Island but again had to turn back. On 12 July there was yet another attempt – again they had to turn back empty handed. On 25 August, Shackleton obtained from the Chilean government a small steamer, the *Yelcho*, not built for navigating through ice but Shackleton judged the weather as good as it was going to get before winter settled in for good. Five days later, 4.5 months after leaving them on the desolate shore, they got near enough to the Island to send small boats to shore. Though some were worse for wear, the men were ready to leave – everyday in August that the sea was clear Wild would order the men to roll up their sleeping bags: 'the boss may come today'. Within one hour, every man that had set out on the *Endurance* was safely aboard and homeward bound.

In his book, Shackleton spends a chapter describing what each man did after their return from Antarctica. It is clear that it was important to him to highlight the participation of most of the men in the war: at the time of his writing, three were killed, five wounded and four decorated. They all seemed to feel some sort of guilt for being on an expedition – no matter how harrowing – while their countrymen fought in the gruesome battlefields of Europe. They cleaned up, rested and fattened up, then left again to use their skills and talents on another expedition, this one to support their countrymen in the name of freedom. Interestingly, several men went on to join other explorations...

The expedition did, ultimately, contribute to the scientific knowledge of the sub-continent and though he did not make his fortune from the experience, he did, most importantly, go down in the annals of history, as he had wanted. He is remembered today not for his failure to cross the South Pole, but for his leadership skills during one of the most gruelling journeys of survival of all time.

9   The mobile lifestyle

Now that you have resettled at your destination, welcome to the mobile lifestyle!

During the course of these chapters, we described the process of moving to live in a new country as more than a relocation from one place to another. To resettle is a process of managing physical, emotional and mental change in order to create a good life for yourself at a new destination. It requires conscious decision-making, self-awareness and an understanding of the phases of resettling in order to lead yourself and your family members to your goal.

    Whether you move once and stay at your destination, move for a short stint abroad and return home, or you continue to make multiple moves, you can now claim to be a modern day explorer. The experience of managing the challenges of leaving home to establish a full life elsewhere will have changed you. You chose to leave the safety of family and friends, the security of routines and the subconscious rules of your community in order to experience the thrill and hardships of discovering a new environment. The experience was a life-changing event. You took a leap from the nest to join a new flock with a different way of life. The bird that returns from the yearly migration is stronger, more independent, with skills that it would not have developed had it stayed at home.

Moving to resettle in a different country tests your skills and determination and requires that you accept that your way of doing things is not the only way. Therefore, people who move tend to have a greater tolerance of others who are different; they have generally become more flexible in their approach to life. People who have lived in other countries see the world differently from those who never leave their country of origin: distances across continents seem shorter and events that affect people far away feel more personal and real. Individuals who have created a good life for themselves in more than one country tend to be resourceful problem-solvers who are dedicated to making their lives and those of their family's and others' around them, positive and enjoyable. They may not always find it easy, but through personal experience they know that perseverance pays off.

As a result of these changes, mobile individuals recognise in each other similarities in their worldview, their values and the expectations, regardless of their nationality or the countries they lived in. This mutual recognition is similar to what happens when two individuals of the same nationality meet while living abroad: they recognise the norms and values of their mutual cultural heritage. In this sense, people who have experienced resettling abroad form a loose network of like-minded individuals that we call the 'mobile tribe.' Members of this tribe tend to have skills, knowledge and attitudes that are effective in dealing with transitions. In this chapter we summarise these in order to highlight their usefulness in dealing with any transition in your life, including, for example, retirement. We also look at two challenges that members of the mobile tribe face because their lifestyle differs from the 'norm': the notion of 'belonging', and the issues faced when returning 'home'.

The mobile profile

We mentioned earlier that intelligence is increasingly recognised to be more than how your brain processes information. Rather than just IQ (what you know or how smart you are), organisations that recruit talented individuals look for elements of the emotional, body, and moral intelligence that are most effective for the job they need to do. In *The Mobile Life*, we described the skills, knowledge and attitudes that best help individuals manage change through each stage of resettling. Here we regroup them according to these four quotients.

Emotional Quotient

Members of the mobile tribe tend to be:

- Aware of their own cultural norms, values and expectations as well as their emotions during periods of change or stress
- Self-motivated in achieving their goals and are able to manage their emotions and choose positive responses
- Empathetic with others and are thereby adept in social relationships and in meeting new people
- Flexible and tolerant of ambiguity and uncertainty
- Appreciative of what they have, live in the present and remain optimistic and positive
- Able to guide others through their change process
- Enthusiastic and positive about taking on adventures and dealing with change

Intelligence quotient

Members of the mobile tribe tend to have:

⟫ An expanded world view in that they have deeper knowledge and understanding of each of the countries they have lived in and know what information they need to gather about their future destination (the physical conditions, socio-political realities and the culture)

⟫ Knowledge of their team members' abilities, expectations and character as well as an understanding of each members' way of dealing with change

⟫ Knowledge of the phases of moving:
  ⟫ Making the decision to move;
  ⟫ Preparing and disengaging;
  ⟫ Arriving and thriving long-term

⟫ Knowledge of the phases of adjustment:
  ⟫ Acclimatisation
  ⟫ Adaptation
  ⟫ Acculturation

⟫ The desire to learn (curiosity and open-mindedness)

Body Quotient

Members of the mobile tribe are conscious of:

- Their physiological needs
- Their culture (values, norms, beliefs, opinions and attitudes)
- Their reaction to differences in others
- Their personal approach to change

Being aware of the skills, knowledge and attitudes that you developed or strengthened as a result of your mobile life will enable you to consciously and with confidence, apply them to any transition in your life. You can, for example, apply the framework of this book to plan for and execute your retirement as a project through change. Furthermore, when approaching future potential employers, awareness of your personal achievements can help you describe, even to individuals who have never experienced an international move, what you have gained from your transition process. This is particularly important for partners who have not worked during their time abroad. For example, even if you have not had paid employment during your time abroad, you can certainly claim to be flexible in dealing with change and uncertainty, to have experience and skills in dealing with people of different cultural and socio-economic backgrounds and have a proven track record in self-motivation and perseverance in achieving your goals.

The notion of belonging

A commonly heard criticism of the mobile lifestyle is that mobile individuals belong 'everywhere and nowhere'. If we return to the

Moral Quotient

Members of the mobile tribe tend to:

- Be self-confident and determined but are humble in recognising and respecting the culture of others
- Have the ability to adjust their behaviour and communication patterns in order to get on with others
- Have a good sense of humour and the ability to keep perspective

idea of 'roots' introduced in Chapter 8, mobile individuals bring their roots, earth and pot with them and therefore can thrive and 'belong' in any environment they are set in, just as an orchid can. Members of the mobile tribe can create a sense of belonging anywhere they choose to settle. Their physical maps have foldaway flaps for each location they have lived in. A section may be faded from disuse but can be re-activated at any moment. Mobile individuals are comfortable with their multiple maps, easily switching from the conditions in one location to another. When they arrive at a new destination, they know the importance of filling in their activity map and establishing relationships on their identity map; they anticipate the discomfort of not having established routines and know how to navigate new territory and social networks, relying on the skills, attitudes and knowledge they've used before.

But the orchid's pot can be an isolating factor in an individual's ability to belong in any given location. If your salary is paid at 'home', you are protected from the vagaries of local economic policy; if you do not speak the local language or live in an enclosed compound, you may create a good life for yourself but will not truly belong in the nation or community you live in. This is particularly the case for the classic expat who is transferred between multiple postings.

As we have said throughout this book, whether you immigrate to a country or move there for only a few years, there is a large degree of choice on your part as to the extent to which you participate in the local or national life. How much effort you make to 'belong' will depend on a) your vision of your good life at your destination, and b) the consequences you personally perceive – both short- and long-term, of not belonging in the country you live in. To what degree do you feel that it is important to your identity or your sense of wellbeing that you 'belong'? The amount of effort you need to make in order to belong will also depend on c) how locals feel about having an outsider live among them. To local people who have not travelled, even after years among them, you may not 'belong' in the same way that others do, especially if you intend to move again. Some people may feel that it is not worth investing in a friendship if you are to leave in a few years.

But the idea of belonging at your current location is not the only issue for mobile individuals: there is also your sense of belonging in your 'home' country.

The issue of returning 'home'

Arguably, the hardest move mobile individuals make is when they return 'home', whether that is after a short period away or an entire career of multiple moves. Whether you return for a holiday or to resettle, mobile individuals often realise that they no longer feel as at 'home' as they did before. There are several reasons for why this sense of alienation occurs.

Firstly, you probably do not expect your return to be hard: it should be easy since you are returning to a known environment. But often, because you haven't prepared in the same way you did when you moved abroad, you come upon unexpected difficulties. In other words you did not anticipate the challenges posed by your move. Secondly, upon returning, you confront directly how you have changed through your experience abroad. You are no longer the person that left. So, for example, you no longer find the same things interesting or the topics of discussion or activities you now enjoy are not available. This can lead to a sense of alienation – you no longer fit in as you did before. Thirdly, not only have you changed, but the people and the place you left may not seem to have changed (or changed little). Also, family and old friends probably expect you to just get on with life as you always did. You were accustomed to being different, perhaps a bit special and thereby interesting while overseas; now you may simply feel like one of many and very far from the mobile tribe that would understand and empathise with your experiences and the challenges you now face in returning home.

Finally, resettlers are explorers and explorers are people who enjoy challenging themselves, getting through hardships and achieving their goals. During expeditions, explorers live intensely in the present and can become addicted to the adrenaline of their sport. Like with Shackleton's crew, some explorers chose to join other expeditions and continue their life of discovery and adventure. To these individuals, 'home' can seem boring in that every aspect is known and navigating is easy.

These challenges can give you the feeling of not belonging, which can be disconcerting. Being aware of what you are going through is important. It is also useful to discern exactly what it is that sets you apart from your local community. What is it, exactly, that makes you feel uncomfortable and how can you deal with each of these issues in turn? Are you missing conversations on international topics? Seek out others who have had similar experiences with whom you can keep up with issues that interested you abroad. Is the pace of life too repetitive? Treat home like a foreign location and discover things you didn't know before. Treat 'returning home' as a relocation to a new place and use the approach we discuss in this book to plan, prepare and manage yourself and your family through the experience.

When you, a member of the mobile tribe, are a minority among non-mobile individuals, you can feel as though your values and preferences are misunderstood or somehow 'wrong'. Remember, however, that you may not conform to the local 'norm', but that is because you have had an enriching experience that broadened your worldview, your values, beliefs and expectations. This 'difference' you share with other members of the mobile tribe – there may even be aspects of your expanded culture that others around can learn or benefit from.

Children, belonging and returning 'home'
This issue of belonging is especially important to parents who raise internationally mobile children. We expect our children to adapt easily to being 'home' but often your 'home' is a totally new country for them. You will, of course, have given your children an upbringing that reflects your national values, norms and expected behaviours. But do not forget that your children are also influenced by their experiences – as we mentioned in the last chapter, your children will likely be different to local children in important ways. This does not need to pose any problems to your children per se – children tend to be adaptable and learn quickly through their desire to 'fit in'. However, if you return 'home' and expect your mobile children to fit in easily, then, you may be surprised to realise that they experience difficulties adjusting. Just as you needed to help them adjust to their new environment abroad, you will need to provide support for their return 'home'.

Parents must be prepared to make an effort to get their kids to feel happily established in your home nation. Your 'overseas' destination may provide advantages that 'home does not, such as a different quality of education, or your children may not have access to the activities, sports etc. that they had at your destination. Furthermore, your kids may experience that their status is different – if a child was one among many mobile children in their old school, they may suddenly find themselves being new and different. Just as with any move to a new environment, they will leave established friendship networks and it will take as much time for them to make friends at home as it did abroad. At home, they may be looked at and treated as 'outsiders': local kids will have different ideas about what is 'cool' in terms of things like clothing, music, television programmes. And because their worldview is different, what the home kids do and talk about may not be the same as what the kids at your destination do and talk about.

Therefore, at the beginning of your return home, you will need to be alert to how your children's transition is going and look for ways to make the process as smooth as possible. If you feel that they need it, try to give them access, even if occasionally, to other mobile children. When resettling at home, remember to plan the process and support them in identifying their vision just as you did when you moved overseas.

A final note

Moving to live in a new country is a major life-changing event. Human beings are resilient: many of us can resettle instinctively, relying on our natural adaptability and problem-solving abilities to resettle abroad. However, even members of the mobile tribe who have experienced multiple moves may not be conscious of the range of abilities they have developed through their experiences. In *The Mobile Life*, we describe the knowledge, skills and attitudes that help you take control of the emotional and psychological effects of this period of transition. Much of this comes from personal and organisational change management as well as leadership theory and is applicable to any area of your private life and your career. Imagining change as an expedition allows you to plan and manage the process of adjustment for yourself and your family members. By reading this book, we hope to have helped you sustain the motivation to create that good life that you imagined at your destination, so that in ten or twenty years' time, when you look back on your adventure, you can be proud of and satisfied with your expedition abroad.

Checklist for preparing your move

Here is a list of items that are intended purely to get you thinking about the elements of your life that need to be dealt with as you disengage from your current location as well as things that help you prepare for your future life.

Research sources

There are many useful resources for information on your destination including:

- ➤ Books
  - ➤ Non-fiction about the country, history, politics...
  - ➤ Travel guides
  - ➤ Fiction by local writers
  - ➤ Books about or for local children
  - ➤ Local recipe books
  - ➤ Picture books of the geography and or peoples
  - ➤ CultureSmart! guides on national cultures
  - ➤ Maps and guidebooks or travel logs

- ➤ Internet
  - ➤ Local government or private sites about living in the country
  - ➤ Travel sites
  - ➤ Blogs or sites from expats

- Information on any topic about the country
- YouTube and other clips of musicians, artists, speakers, politicians...
- Local sites of cultural organisations like museums etc.
- Mobile apps for devices such as Googlemaps, Wikihood, AroundMe, Wikipanion

- Audio-visual material like documentaries or films
  - About the country
  - Films set in the country
  - Locally made films (in translation if necessary)

Car

- Sell or rent or transfer it to your new location
- Car registration and insurance in your current and future locations
- Car or road taxes or licences
- Parking permits

Children

Many groups will need to be informed of the departure of your children, including:

- The current school (and registration in the future school)
- Clubs, classes, subscriptions they may belong to
- Their friends and acquaintances

Your current home

If you own your home, there will be a different list of action items depending on whether you decide to rent or sell your home, or leave it empty. You could be dealing with

- Estate agents

- Taxes, insurance...
- An inventory of your belongings that you are taking with you and/or leaving behind

And there are connections to be terminated:

- From national or municipal registries
- From service providers (gas, electricity, telephone, Internet, cable/satellite TV

Finance
A few elements you may need to deal with are:

- Automatic payments
- Credit card validity for at least 3 months after departure date and usable at your destination
- Taxation issues

Health
Beyond having health insurance that is appropriate for your destination, you may need to deal with the following:

- Your GP, dentist, optician and orthodontist and ask for your records or get medical check-ups and inoculations
- Spare glasses or a supply of lenses
- A basic medical kit

Mail and communication
- Redirection of mail including magazine or newspaper subscriptions
- Change of address notifications to your network (banks, insurance companies, investment companies, Embassy/Consulate, personal contacts and business contacts of your change of address)

- Save your contact list in both soft copy and print-out
- There may be changes to your e-mail account or other online services as well as mobile phone accounts

Miscellaneous

- Organise a going away party for yourself

Packing

What you bring with you will depend on the phases of your move. You may need to move out of your home and into temporary accommodation at your current and future locations. You may bring only suitcases, and/or air shipment and/or larger sea freight so that your belongings will arrive at different speeds. In your planning, remember:

- The paperwork you need to have at your destination (birth and marriage certificates, drivers licence, school reports, insurance documents, reference letters, CV, inventories visa applications etc.)
- The paperwork (bills etc.) you need regarding your current location
- Passports that are valid for at least 6 months after your departure date
- The items that you and your children need to have during the various phases of your travels from the moment your leave your current to the time you are resettled at your destination

Pets

If your pet(s) will travel with you, you will need to arrange medical checks, travel arrangements and research care and conditions at your destination.

Removals

You may need to select a removal company and take with you:

- A copy of the removal contract and contact details
- A copy of removal inventory
- Perhaps keep pictures of any particularly valuables like furniture or artwork
- Perhaps purchase receipts of particular items

Notes

ALEXANDER, C (1998), The Endurance: Shackleton's legendary Antarctic Expedition, New York: Alfred A. Knopf Publisher

HALL, ET (1997) *Beyond Culture*, New York: Anchor Books

JENSEN, K (2012), "Intelligence is overrated: What you really need to succeed", *Forbes.com*, [Online at http://www.forbes.com/sites/keldjensen/2012/04/12/intelligence-is-overrated-what-you-really-need-to-succeed/]

LANSING, A (1999), *Endurance: Shackleton's Incredible Voyage* (2nd edition), New York: Basic Books

MASLOW, A (1970), *Motivation and Personality*, 2nd ed., New York: Harper & Row

SHACKLETON, SIR E (1998), *South*, Guilford: The Lyons Press

Further Reading

Culture

BENNETT, MJ (2004), "Becoming interculturally competent", in J.S. Wurzel (Ed.) *Toward multiculturalism: A reader in multicultural education*, Newton, MA: Intercultural Resource Corporation

CORNES, A (2004), *Culture from the Inside Out: Travel and Meet Yourself*, Yarmouth, ME: Intercultural Press

GEERT HOFSTEDE, G, GJ HOFSTEDE AND M MINKOV (2010), *Cultures and Organizations: Software of the Mind*, 3rd Edition, New York: The McGraw-Hill Companies

LEWIS, RD (2000), *When Cultures Collide,* London: Nicholas Brealey Publishing

MARX, E (2001), *Breaking through Culture Shock: What You Need to Succeed in International Business*, London: Nicholas Brealey Publishing

STORTI, C (2001), *The Art of Crossing Cultures*, London: Nicholas Brealey Publishing

TROMPENAARS, F AND C HAMPDEN-TURNER (2011), *Riding the Waves of Culture: Understanding Diversity in Global Business*, New York: The McGraw-Hill Companies

YON, DA (2000), *Elusive Culture: Schooling, Race, and Identity in Global Times*, New York: State University of New York Press

Culture shock

KEALEY, DJ (1989), A study of *cross-cultural effectiveness: theoretical issues, practical applications*, International Journal of Intercultural Relations 13:3 p 387-428

WARD, C, S BOCHNER AND A FURNHAM (2001), *The Psychology of Culture Shock* (2nd edition), London: Routledge

Families moving abroad

ALI, AJ (2003), *The Intercultural adaptation of expatriate spouses and children: An empirical study on the determinants contributing to the success of expatriation*, El Sobrante, California: Labyrinth Publication

BRYSON, D AND C HOGE (2003), *A portable identity: a woman's guide to maintaining a sense of self while moving overseas*, Maryland: Transition Press International

HART, DR R (2012), *Preparing for your move abroad*, London: Kuperard

LINDERMAN, P AND M HESS-BRAYER (2002), *Expert Expat: Your Guide to Successful Relocation Abroad – Moving, Living, Thriving*, London: Nicholas Brealey Publishing

MALEWSKI, M (2005) *GenXpat: the young professional's guide to making a successful life abroad*, Yarmouth, ME: Intercultural Press

PASCOE, R (1003) *Culture Shock! Successful living abroad: a wife's guide*, North Vancouver, BC: Expatriate Press

QUICK,TL (2010), *The Global Nomad's Guide to University Transition*, Summertime Publishing, 2010

Intercultural issues

KNIGHT, JM AND RL KOHLS (1994), *Developing Intercultural Awareness: A Cross-Cultural Training Handbook,* London: Nicholas Brealey Publishing

PETERSON, B (2004) *Cultural Intelligence: A Guide to Working with People from Other Cultures,* London: Nicholas Brealey Publishing

SPENCER-OATEY, H AND P FRANKLIN (2009), *Intercultural Interaction: a multidisciplinary approach to intercultural communication,* London: Palgrave Macmillan

VULPE, T, D KEALEY, D PROTHEROE AND D MACDONALD (2001), *A profile of the interculturally effective person,* Centre for Intercultural Learning, [Online at http://www.international.gc.ca/cfsi-icse/cil-cai/pubpap-pubdoc-eng.asp]

Moving with children

JUDITH M. BLOHM, JM (1996), *Where in the World are You Going?,* London: Nicholas Brealey Publishing

PASCOE, R (2006), *Raising Global Nomads: Parenting Abroad in an On-Demand World,* North Vancouver, BC: Expatriate Press

Pollock, D and R Van Reken, *Third Culture Kids: The Experience of Growing Up Among Worlds,* London; Nicholas Brealey Publishing

VAN SWOL-ULBRICH, H AND B KALTENHÄUSER (2002), *When abroad do as the local children do,* The Netherlands: XPat Media

Organisational change management

KANE, W (2008), *The Truth About Managing Change*, New Jersey: Prentice Hall

SCOTT, C (2004), *Managing Personal Change: Moving Through Personal Transition*, Mississauga, Ontario: Crisp Learning

Personal transition and change

BRIDGES, W (1991), *Managing transitions; making the most of change*, Reading, Massachusetts: Addison-Wesley Publishing Company

BRIDGES, W (2004) *Transitions-Making sense of life's changes*, Reading, Massachusetts: Da Capo Press

GOLEMAN, D (1998), *Working with Emotional Intelligence*, New York: Bantam Books

JOHNSON, DR S (1998), *Who Moved My Cheese?*, London: Vermillion

SCOTT, CD, AND DT JAFFE (2004), *Managing personal change: moving through personal transition*, New York: Axzo Press